LEARNING TO LOVE

PASSION, COMPASSION AND THE ESSENCE OF THE GOSPEL

HEIDI AND ROLLAND BAKER

Chosen

a division of Baker Publishing Group
Minneapolis, Minnesota

Originally published by River Publishing and Media Ltd., Maidstone, Kent, United Kingdom.

Published by Chosen Books
11400 Hampshire Avenue South
Bloomington, Minnesota 55438
www.chosenbooks.com

Chosen Books is a division of
Baker Publishing Group, Grand Rapids, Michigan

Printed in the United States of America

Library of Congress Cataloging-in-Publication Data

Baker, Heidi.
    Learning to love: passion, compassion and the essence of the gospel / Heidi and Rolland Baker.
       p.   cm.
    Summary: "Through powerful, poignant stories, bestselling authors reveal behind-the-scenes glimpses of their ministry in Mozambique—and what they have learned about, and from, the Holy Spirit"—Provided by publisher.
    ISBN 978-0-8007-9552-8 (pbk. : alk. paper)
    1. Church work with children—Mozambique. 2. Missions—Mozambique. 3. Baker, Heidi. 4. Baker, Rolland. I. Baker, Rolland. II. Title.
BV2616.B28 2013
266'.02322679—dc23   2012040228

The internet addresses, email addresses, and phone numbers in this book are accurate at the time of publication. They are provided as a resource. Baker Publishing Group does not endorse them or vouch for their content or permanence.

Cover design by Lookout Design, Inc.

13 14 15 16 17 18 19   7 6 5 4 3 2 1

Contents

Foreword

Learning to Love is a compelling story of the day-to-day workings of one of the world's most amazing ministries through one of the world's most amazing couples. Church history testifies to this fact. And thankfully, it's happening now, not hundreds of years ago. The setting is Mozambique, Africa, where everything seems to be experienced in the extreme.

This book has been birthed out of a life of deep contrasts—great suffering and great joy, extreme poverty and supernatural supply, tragic loss followed by great gain and advancement. There has been so much opposition and persecution, so much loss and daily opportunity for discouragement and giving up. But you won't find that theme here. This book is a book of victory, healings, salvations, overcoming insurmountable odds and the continuous celebration and joy in the goodness of God that meets every need presented.

Rolland and Heidi Baker's impact on my life is hard to articulate without sounding careless with flattery. Yet everything I could say is understated. They illustrate the fullness of Jesus' life and ministry in a greater measure than is normally seen or heard of in our day.

All the elements that make up a true kingdom lifestyle of significance are theirs and are increasing—the sheer number of conversions, transformation of society, purity in heart and life and demonstrations of power, including resurrections from the dead. All these things testify of the wonder of the Lord Jesus Christ working in and through them. Their impact on Mozambique is legendary, especially considering the measure of darkness that overshadowed that nation when the Bakers arrived so many years ago. But though these measurements may provide a legitimate standard for examining their "success," their outstanding feature is unquestionably love. Hence, the title of this book: *Learning to Love*. Everything listed above flows from this one thing—love. They love. And they love well.

Simply put, *Learning to Love* raises the bar on our understanding of the normal Christian life. Rolland and Heidi Baker would be the first to tell us that they are normal believers with an extraordinary God, and what they do is meant to be the norm. The simplicity of their devotion to Christ is alarming. And the measure of power that they and their team live in is breathtaking.

Because of this, much happens out in the bush with tribes that have never before heard the Gospel. The setting is almost always dangerous, from the treacherous roads, to flying to remote villages, to finding a way across the sea in a boat to reach the unreached, to the angry witch doctors who are threatened by their presence. The day-to-day takes on a whole new meaning as you are taken on the adventure of giving the Gospel to hungry people in remote places and seeing the goodness of God demonstrated time and time again. Healings happen easily, and so many have come to the Lord because of this willing and giving ministry. Life as usual pales in the light of these stories. This book stirs up a hunger for the "more"—at any cost.

Rolland and Heidi Baker have not tried to deviate from the standard or example that Jesus gave us. Love is supreme. Settling for life without power is unacceptable. Going into the darkest places on earth to find the lost is the mandate: no excuses. This is how they live. And we are the better for it.

Bill Johnson, Bethel Church, Redding, California; author,
Hosting the Presence and *When Heaven Invades Earth*

Introduction

Hong Kong, the late '80s. Having begun Iris Ministries in 1980 in the United States as a short-term missions organization reaching out to the Philippines, and later basing ourselves in Indonesia, Rolland and I were eventually denied permanent missionary visas and found ourselves on a plane to Hong Kong, where we would minister for the next few years.

Walking through the backstreets one day, far from the bright lights and bustling thoroughfares of downtown, I saw a small girl huddled in an alleyway. She was lost, alone, dirty and abandoned. The thought struck me: *If I don't pause to show this girl even the smallest, most basic act of kindness, then who will?* She wasn't crying out, demanding my attention or making a fuss. It would have been so easy to just keep walking, look the other way, go about my business. . . .

London, England, the early '90s. Rolland and I moved to England to study for our PhDs at the University of London. In this vast, sprawling conurbation we found the same paradox: incredible wealth living shoulder to shoulder with utter poverty and desperation. In London this can somehow co-exist in areas barely one street apart—or even at opposite ends of the same street!

In no time at all we were confronted with the need we had encountered on the streets of Hong Kong. A homeless man was roaming the streets. He had lived another life in Eastern Europe as a celebrated concert pianist. He had left everything and moved to London to further his career. But the expected connections never made good, doors of opportunity shut in his face and his finances dwindled. Before he knew it, he had nothing; no credentials in this city and no way of returning to his former life. I saw him sitting in a doorway, lost in his thoughts, wondering how circumstances had conspired to bring him to this. He reminded me of the little girl in Hong Kong; he had that same faraway look of resigned hopelessness.

Someone had to do something. We began a church among the homeless, which we ran for the duration of our doctoral studies. We were determined that the *homeless* should not also be the *hopeless*.

Mozambique, the mid-'90s. We arrived in Mozambique in 1995 and it has been the focus of our ministry ever since. One day I came across a young girl by the roadside. She was a ten-year-old with one leg missing, which she had lost in a house fire. Being of "no use" to anyone as an amputee, her grandmother had ordered her brothers to stone her to death in a field. One less mouth to feed. They left her for dead, but she somehow survived. Now she was living on the street, selling her body for the price of a soda or a mouthful of bread. It broke my heart to see her and I was faced with that question again: *Who will stop for this one? Who will make a difference in her life? Who will be the hands of Jesus to her?*

This little girl, Elaina, taught me that *love looks like something*. What is love if it does not look like something—a comforting word, an offer of help, something to eat, clothes to wear? This is the Gospel.

I realize that reading this account of what God is doing in Mozambique can seem terrifying, overwhelming and somewhat detached from the day-to-day reality of life for many.

Or is it?

If there is one thing I have learned it is this: Poverty and desperation do not always look the way we expect. There are countless thousands in our world who need someone to stop for them, someone to show them God's kindness and mercy. Never let the fact that they wear suits and drive nice cars fool you—nor the fact that they appear to have their lives together. Simmering just below the surface is the same hopelessness and despair that lived in the eyes of the girl in the alleyway, the man in the doorway, the girl by the roadside; they have simply learned to disguise it. There are people in need where you are, just as there are people in need where I am.

Another thing I have learned: *I am not qualified to do what I do!* I am far from perfect. In and of myself, I can do nothing. It is only Christ in me that empowers me to stop for the one, and then do something practical for that person. But I have found that as I make the decision simply to stop and pay attention, Jesus unleashes miraculous power beyond my imagining.

This is how I know, without doubt, that He can do the same through you. If He can use me, He can use anyone. Jesus can use you to be an example of His love wherever you are and whatever you do. Whether you work in a store, for a bank, at a hospital, in an office . . . as you learn to surrender your life to Him more and more, He *will* touch lives through you and you *will* see miracles. You may not need a miracle of food multiplication in your situation. But you may need the miracle of hard hearts softened and relationships transformed. You may need the miracles of emotional brokenness healed and wholeness restored.

Wherever you find yourself on your journey with God today, please know that He can use *you* to do something amazing. All that is required is a simple act of obedience on your part. Do what only you can do—because you are there!—and God will do what only He can do.

Heidi Baker, 2012

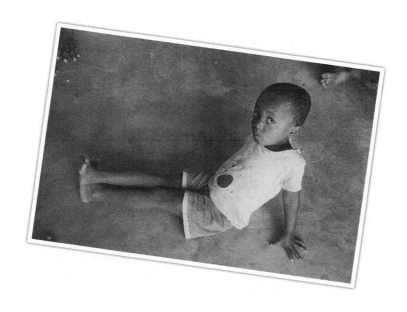

Preface

The glistening blue-green ocean could not be any more beautiful. Gleaming, wet children are running, leaping and doing cartwheels all the way up and down the beach. Many others are splashing and diving into the water. Palm trees and cumulus clouds drift softly in the gentle breeze to complete the impression of *freedom, peace and joy*. Today we are celebrating all the birthdays of the month of our Iris Ministries family here in Pemba and our students' success in school.

After hours of play we all gather to distribute gifts. Each birthday child and top student gets a colorful bag full of presents. Then we line everyone up for cake and soft drinks. From two-year-olds to teenagers, everyone is enjoying a rich day together.

It is both our calling and our inheritance to bring His life to the homeless, the desperately poor and forgotten. Their beautiful, beaming smiles are the reward Jesus gives us. We love bringing salvation *to the least of these*. Without the power of God we could not exist here. Every celebration drink and bag of gifts is made possible by the miraculous generosity of God's people.

Our missionary and Mozambican teams are heroes to us. Our passion and compassion are ignited by the Holy Spirit. Our health and sustenance come from Him. Our hope for all these children comes from the Gospel alone. For us, every day is a celebration of our life in Jesus. *Thank you* for celebrating with us!

PART 1

PASSION AND COMPASSION

1

The Great Wedding Feast

*"Lord, I'm asking You to wreck my
heart and to make it bigger."*

Heidi: We are profoundly grateful for everyone around the world who remembers us in our beloved Mozambique. We receive support from all around the world, which goes to feed the hungry people here that Jesus has asked us to feed—both spiritually and physically. It amazes me how God has raised up such faithful ones to assist in accomplishing His work. They are our beloved and extended family, and we so appreciate the prayers, love and extravagant gifts for the poor that every person contributes.

Recently, the Lord has been speaking to me from the parable of the Great Banquet in Luke 14. I had the honor of hosting more than four thousand guests at the wedding of our daughter, Crystalyn Joy, to Brock Human. It was a glorious, beautiful day with the sunshine shimmering on the stunning turquoise Indian Ocean.

Our daughter, Crystalyn, on her wedding day

Rolland walked Crystalyn down the sandy aisle. A sea of African children, all singing, streamed down from the streets and joined in the bridal procession. Pastor José from Maputo and Pastor José from Pemba— our coastal town of some fifty thousand people in the northern province of Cabo Delgado— helped me officiate the wedding ceremony.

Crystalyn and Brock stood under a massive bougainvillea wedding arch. The wedding was set on the beach right across from our "Village of Joy," and 64 of our Mozambican children comprised the bridal party. They looked fabulously colorful in their blue and yellow *kapelanas* and African shirts.

The reception was filled with praise and dancing. Hundreds of pastors and our Harvest School of Missions students served at the wedding feast, dishing out plates heaped with rice, chicken and salad, with cold Coke to drink. The prime minister of Mozambique, business leaders and the poor all ate together. Every one of our four thousand guests received a piece of cake. Many of them ate cake for the first time in their lives. What fun to watch their smiles as all were fed! Food was served for hours. We had commissioned every student and missionary to be baking cakes for days on end.

All of us felt we should model this wedding feast after Luke 14:13: "When you give a banquet, invite the poor, the crippled, the lame, the blind, and you will be blessed." We printed invitations and, just as in Luke 14:21, we went "out quickly into the streets and alleys of the town." After doing this, I was delighted to learn that we still had room, so then we went out to the roads and remote villages, calling people to come so that our church would be filled.

God longs for His house to be filled. He is calling His servant-lovers to run out and call in the poor to His incredibly beautiful wedding feast. He paid for this banquet with His own Son's life, so that all of us could eat. It was a delight to see our new church building filled to overflowing, with everyone enjoying this great wedding day. I felt God smiling on the service as our daughter was married during the most stunning Mozambican sunset.

Family Ties

I love having my natural-born children and family with me this summer. Last week, together as one big family, we rode off to the "bush bush" to preach the Gospel. For the uninitiated, the "bush" in Mozambique is the remote, hard-to-reach places. We have explored the bush, now God is calling us into the "bush bush"—the places where hardly any living souls have cared to venture before.

Over potholes, through fields and unpaved roads, we bounced along for hours singing in my Land Rover, one of a small convoy of vehicles. We love bringing the Good News to the ends of the

Reenacting the parable of the Good Samaritan

earth. Later, in the African night, we pulled into an unreached village where only sixty people had even heard of the name of Jesus.

I climbed up on our four-ton truck, our makeshift preaching platform, as the night began. My spiritual sons and daughters performed a drama about the Good Samaritan. I used this passage to invite the village to meet my Friend—the One who stopped for us—King Jesus. I preached my heart out and loved watching the crowds raise their hands in response. They wanted God! A deaf girl heard, many others were healed and the fame of His name went out from that village.

The village chief was overwhelmed with joy and asked us to open a children's center in his village. He called all the village elders together the next morning to meet with me. He himself had given his life to the Lord in his mud hut as I shared about the beauty of Jesus. We camped out in tents and sleeping bags underneath the African stars, gathering around a campfire as the Mozambican student-pastors shared their testimonies with our mission-school students. Early in the morning we serenaded Brock for his 21st birthday. What a wonderful and unusual way to spend a birthday! The next morning we drove our vehicles to the beach to baptize the new converts.

On the way to the ocean, one of my spiritual sons, Herbert, got his Land Rover stuck in the mud. He had spent two months last year during our terrible floods driving his Land Rover across Mozambique to help feed the fifty thousand people facing starvation. But today—a clear and sunny day—his vehicle was stuck in the mud for six hours! The tide was coming in, so it took a small village to rescue us. Twenty-six new Makua friends (the Makua are the largest ethnic group in northern Mozambique) gathered around the car for hours, working as a team to pull the vehicle out of the mud.

Being dug out of the mud

If the Land Rover had not been stuck, they might not have gotten saved. Jesus stopped for us. We stopped for them. But then they stopped for us! I loved not only giving to the villages, but also receiving from them. We needed their help, and we all worked as one big family, pulling the Land Rover out. We did it together in Jesus. Surely, He lifts us up from our miry pits to set our feet on solid ground. We gave the villagers a gift of three solar-powered New Testament audio players, which they will listen to every night.

I learn so much from my Mozambican friends in their villages and mud huts. I come as a learner first. Then I have the joy of watching them meet Jesus. Village after village is meeting Him and being shaken by the power of His love. We want to invite an entire nation to this wedding feast.

Into His Love

Rolland: One week after the outreach Heidi just described, we set out again in our Land Rovers and four-ton truck—this time to a village that had never heard the Gospel at all. No one in the village knew the name of Jesus.

Somehow we had missed this village, even after planting 670 churches in this "unreachable" province of Cabo Delgado since we arrived five years ago. But once more a deaf-mute was healed and the entire village was electrified and turned to Jesus.

In this case Heidi prayed for the deaf young man and suddenly he could hear. He had neither heard nor spoken a word in his entire life. With his newly found voice he began to imitate Heidi's syllables and the crowd went wild. Everyone knew this man and they knew this had to be God. Clapping, laughing and cheering, the crowd hoisted him up onto their shoulders. Hope came to this village, to every hungry, childlike heart.

The next morning we got down to business and bought a piece of land on which to construct a church building. We will send them a pastor and bring potential leaders among them to one of our Harvest Bible Schools to be trained. Now the village is part of a larger family, and we pray that mercy and grace, power and glory will rain down on its people without measure. They will need much teaching and discipling—something that happens when missionaries take time to visit villages and spend

Deaf and mute from birth, he is now hearing and speaking

one-on-one time with the people. This is where the most spiritual progress is made.

It Starts with a Question

Heidi: Jesus loves us so much that He *never* leaves us the way He finds us. His love often starts with a question—a question that reaches down from the safety of our minds, right into our hearts. *Do you love Me?*

Often we are too quick to answer when God asks us a question. Usually, our hearts have not fully grasped what He wants us to understand. God is looking to affect our hearts more than our minds. He wants to *wreck* our hearts—to change the way our hearts feel and react to the situations that exist in a broken world.

Do you love Me? Will you complete your work? Will you fulfill your destiny because of who Jesus is? That is the only reason to do anything, beloved, and it is the only safe place to be—in Him, drinking Him, imbibing Him over and over; to be filled and poured out, filled and poured out.

Day and night Jesus is the Bread and the Wine that sustains me. He is everything I need. Unless I have more of Him, I cannot function. I do not have a backup plan. Some speakers can pull out their laptops and show amazing PowerPoint presentations. I am not being facetious when I say that these things really *do* impress me. I always say "Wow!" when I see them. But that is not me. I can barely operate a computer. There are many things I am not good at—but I do have *passion* for the Presence of Jesus. The cry of my heart is: *God, unless You show up, I'll die!* I am a desperate person.

Scripture says, "Love the Lord your God with all your mind." We are called to love God with every fiber of our being. All of us, in our entirety, must be wholly given over to the Master—our hearts, our souls, our minds, our emotions. God wants us to be fully yielded to Him. To "love the Lord your God with all your heart and with all your soul and with all your strength and with all your mind"—this is passion. Why would any of us want to go to one more church meeting if we did not possess this kind of passion? I confess: I do not like church! Unless God shows up, I do not like it. Without Him it is almost entirely pointless, isn't it?

Let us determine to live a life abandoned to His love—a life made up of passion. Decide to trade the worst for the best, death for life, darkness for light.

> But whatever was to my profit I now consider loss for the sake of Christ. What is more, I consider everything a loss compared to the surpassing greatness of knowing Christ Jesus my Lord, for whose sake I have lost all things. I consider them rubbish, that I may gain Christ.
>
> Philippians 3:7–8

In surrender we actually lose nothing. We stand only to gain. We are gaining a life lived in His love. I pray that we will lay down our little lives in His love, like tiny seeds, asking Him to water us with the Spirit of the Living God—seeds that are planted to bring forth life as He shows us how to live.

An oak tree starts life as an acorn hidden in the dirt. Nobody would even know it was there. But contained within that tiny, hidden thing are all the makings of beauty, might, splendor and shelter. The little acorn simply takes a lifetime to become all that it was always meant to be.

Before anything else, beloved, we are His, hidden in Him.

Time to Reflect

When they had finished eating, Jesus said to Simon Peter, "Simon son of John, do you truly love me more than these?" "Yes, Lord," he said, "you know that I love you." Jesus said, "Feed my lambs."

John 21:15

2

Living on the Edge

*"What is it going to take for me
to know eternal life?"*

Rolland: These are exciting times. Despite the worst that Satan can do, our family and our churches in several provinces of Mozambique continue to grow in number and strength. The Kingdom of God is upon us. The power of heaven is breaking into our world on earth. We stay filled by feeding on the Word of God and then doing what it says. In so doing we draw close to our Savior—so close that even our wildest imagination cannot keep up with the wonder of our relationship with the Son of God.

Each day, and through each trial, the Holy Spirit carries us closer still to our perfect companion, Jesus, the precise image of the Father, whose Son has become our greatest joy. Yes, Jesus forever will be our destination, our purpose for living. "How can we know Him better?" has become the constant cry of our hearts as we increasingly partake of His heavenly nature. From glory to glory we are being transformed by the power of the cross, becoming prepared for an eternity of perfect fellowship with our God.

Often people want to know how to follow us into the mission field, how to be prepared, how to "do" this. All we can say is that our pursuit of His Kingdom has always taken us to the edge. We have never been able to find life by backing away from the edge and leading a more "normal" ministry lifestyle.

Sometimes our flesh cries for more time out—more time to organize our lives and possessions, more time to battle the chaos in our surroundings. Our daily crises demand awareness of the schemes of Satan and ever-increasing trust in our perfect Savior. That means time, lots of time, with Him, talking over everything in our lives. And from our walk with Him we receive the urgency to press on, to run the race, to love our God with all our hearts, with all our strength. And so with every decision, every outlay, every project we start, we move closer to the edge. We already live in an impossible realm, but Jesus sends us teams, support, ideas and initiative, and we go on, pressing forward to what lies ahead.

Our journey takes us to those who have fallen over the edge and need rescuing—the poor, the homeless, the orphans. They know they are in great need of practical and spiritual help, and they are not too proud to receive. Once they see love—real love from the Master Himself—in our lives, they come to the King. Entire villages come to Jesus when they see that He heals the deaf and blind with just a touch and a word. When we bring a truckload of food for a feast, or handheld solar-panel units that play recordings of the Bible, or new Bibles for the pastors, or clothes, or plastic to waterproof thatched roofs, the love of God flows freely. Then Heidi and I find ourselves right up against the edge and it is time for our spirits to be replenished.

Solar-powered NT player for pastors whose reading skills are marginal

We cannot leave the edge because we see that so much more is needed. These villages are parched. People walk for hours to get water, carrying it in jugs on their heads. Our older youth need simple block houses to live in, now that they have outgrown our children's homes. We need to buy property and a building in downtown Maputo for a church center. We need honest and capable construction workers who can build our primary school before the rainy season. We need to diffuse and heal the serious tensions that exist between northern and southern tribes in Mozambique. And we need to demonstrate to the Muslims all around us that we are here for love, pure love from God.

We are here to demonstrate the Kingdom in every way we can. We need to be so full of the Spirit that our service to the King is exhilarating. For that we need provision of every kind—the kind of provision that we do not see unless we are here, living on the edge.

We invite you, beloved of God, to live on the edge, too. That means something different for each person, because you are made just for Him. But I pray you will know the *edge* that God is calling *you* to live on. What does this mean in practice, in your everyday life? Loving God with all your heart, mind, soul and strength will take you to the end of yourself and you will find yourself looking out over a precipice. You know you are in the place God wants you when only He can keep you from falling.

Only faith working through love counts. Let's never leave behind the simplicity and purity of devotion to Jesus. All we can know when the pressure becomes great is Jesus and Him crucified. We exist by the power of the cross, safe and secure there. From our position at the foot of the cross we warn and persuade to the limit of our ability the multitudes that pass by. Those who turn and follow us into the heart of Jesus will be our joy forever.

Moving Mountains

Heidi: We have had a very challenging and powerful month. So much has happened that when I consider the past few weeks, it feels as though an entire year has gone by. We have dealt with tribal conflicts and governmental controversies. We have built and dedicated several new churches, and we have also had a church and home confiscated by local, corrupt government officials. Three of our pastors were beaten for the sake of the Gospel. A group from another religion was furious that we were sharing our faith. Even though we were ministering on our property, outside our own church, they started to stone our trucks and pulled our pastor, Carlos, off by the neck to beat him. One of our youth leaders, Dilo, ran in front of the angry group that was coming after me so that I could get away with Rolland and our friends Georgian and Winnie Banov in our Land Rover. I felt the power of God's love through the immense courage of our young leaders!

After long hours of discussion and many days of prayer, things have begun to feel a little more peaceful. One Sunday,

31

as I shared how we chose as a church body to forgive those who attacked us because of the love of Christ Jesus, right then a Muslim man came to the front to say he wanted this Jesus because he had seen His love in action. He then called forward his wife and five children in plain daylight to receive Christ as their Savior. The police later captured some of the angry mob who had beaten our pastors. We were called in to the station so that the detainees could be charged and put behind bars. We let them go instead, pleading with them not to burn down our church. Love covers all things. We believe His love will fill us, even in the most difficult of circumstances.

The next night we went right back out on another outreach and four deaf people were healed. One of the older men had been totally deaf for more than twenty years. Word of his healing went back to the religious leaders of the village, who were astonished by such a miracle. They then welcomed us into their village.

A man healed of deafness

There are days when I do not think I can make it for another moment. Then I build myself up in the Lord by remembering all He has done and by looking into the eyes of a precious child, redeemed by His love, whom I am privileged to hold in my arms.

Whenever we go into Cabo Delgado the children seem so hungry for God. We were really encouraged by the visit to Mozambique of our dear friends Georgian and Winnie. Their awesome team paid for a big goat feast and all the children squeezed into the mud hut church to enjoy the tasty meal. Jesus is good all the time, and He has called us to pour out our lives in this very challenging and fruitful nation.

Food Multiplication!

We want to share this encouraging testimony from Juliana Calcado, a Brazilian working with Iris Ministries in Tete, a hot and dry province up against Malawi's arid southern border.

We were visiting the village of Thapo near the border of Malawi. This area is very dry and there are no water wells; water must be carried every day from the river, thirty minutes' walking distance away. The people are extremely desperate for food and water in this place.

Thapo has no electricity or cell phone service, so we could not give notice that we were coming. This is a truly isolated, tremendously needy area of Mozambique.

We thought we had loaded eighteen bags of corn in our truck, but on the way we discovered that we had miscounted and had brought only fourteen bags. There was no food to buy in Thapo and we did not have enough fuel to go back to the storehouse. The stark consequence of arriving in Thapo, four bags short, would mean many children would have to go without a much-needed meal.

As we started giving out the food we gave our worries to the Lord, blessed the meal and focused on the task at hand. As we gave, God multiplied the corn and each of the children received his or her portion! We even had an extra portion to give to a widow who came pleading for leftovers.

It is amazing how God showed up in this desperate situation and how He truly loves His children. His ways are so creative and He is delighted to let us to be His hands and feet in this world!

Love and Power

When you are in love, you are different. You will do anything, go anywhere. All you want is to be with the one you love. This is *passion*: being totally committed, not just dipping your toes into the water to see what the temperature is like. If you are not in love, why serve, why minister, why turn up at church, why go to another meeting?

We had been missionaries for 26 years before we discovered this truth. Rolland was even born on the mission field. But we got really tired and burned out. At one point I used to dream of taking a "normal" job at a store or shop. When we were missionaries in Hong Kong, it was almost like a contest to see who could be the most miserable of His servants. Remember when Jesus called His disciples with the words, "Follow Me"? At the time our version of this was: "Come and follow Me! Be a missionary! Hate the country, hate the climate, hate the customs, hate the food. Come and follow Me! It's fabulous!"

To say we were missing the point is an understatement. But then God got hold of us and poured His sweet "Holy Spirit love" into us. He transformed us into people who are fully in love, fully committed—and with that love comes unstoppable energy. People who know they are loved are trusting people. This is what the apostle Paul, a man who fell in love with Jesus and lived on the edge forever after, wanted for you and me when he wrote these words: "I pray that you, being rooted and established in love, may have power."

When you are in love you have power; you will do anything and go anywhere that your loved one asks. You simply trust the one you love to be there for you. You can run headlong into the dark places if you know that light is waiting for you. You can jump out of a boat into a stormy sea, you can take extravagant risks, you can live right on the edge. If you fall off or fall over, you fall into grace.

I was once at a meeting with a very dignified man of God from Germany. He had a beautiful message. When it was my turn to speak, all I had to say through the Holy Spirit was this: "Too big, too small."

For about twenty minutes all I felt compelled to say, over and over, was just that—"Too big, too small"—until the dignified man of God could not stand it anymore and would have left if God had not stuck him in his chair! (We are good friends now, by the way.) What did this strange message mean? When your mind is *too big* and your heart is *too small*, you cannot get anywhere. You cannot fly, let alone soar.

> "I tell you the truth, if you have faith as small as a mustard seed, you can say to this mountain, 'Move from here to there,' and it will move. Nothing will be impossible for you."
>
> Matthew 17:20

Where does the kind of faith that soars come from? It comes from love, from knowing who Jesus is, from understanding what He thinks of you and realizing who He has made you to be. When you are in love you have power. When you start to grasp how wide and long and high and deep is the love of Christ, you start to get full of God and full of the understanding that whatever He asks you to do, you can do; that wherever He asks you to go, you can go. You can live on the edge, because even in the darkest places, light is waiting there for you. His love, His light in you and me. Passion: It makes us unstoppable.

Too big, too small. Today and for every tomorrow, let's continue to look from earth up toward heaven, to Jesus, and live His love with every breath, that we may be filled to the measure of all the fullness of God. There is nothing impossible about that!

Time to Reflect

And I pray that you, being rooted and established in love, may have power, together with all the saints, to grasp how wide and long and high and deep is the love of Christ, and to know this love that surpasses knowledge—that you may be filled to the measure of all the fullness of God.

Ephesians 3:17–19

3

Groundbreaking News!

*"Come, all you who are thirsty,
come to the waters."*

Rolland: Victory at last! After years of praying, planning, crying, working and networking, on this God-sent day, Friday, September 12, 2008, we broke ground on our big, bold and beautiful well-drilling rig at our Pemba base (one of thirty Iris bases worldwide at this writing). Now we can rejoice together!

We know that the daily lives of hundreds of thousands of people will be transformed by this development. Just as Jesus brought dignity and eternal life to the Samaritan woman when He stopped at the well and asked her for a drink of water, so He will bring dignity to the poor and eternal life to the lost in Mozambique as we drill well after well.

As we break through the hard and dusty ground, we will bring His help and His Good News into the villages. Many of our Mozambican friends walk anywhere from two hours to an entire day just to get one container of water. Many men, women and children die each year from diseases connected to either lack of clean water or contaminated water.

Our heart's desire is to drill a well in each and every village here. Now that our small drill rig is helped by this new rig with its powerful rock blaster, we will be able to cut the cost of drilling bore holes by nearly two-thirds.

Auxiliary truck for pumping water down through the drill bit

In position for drilling

Not only was it unusually expensive to hire outside well-drilling companies to do this work, but also it became impossible in northern Mozambique even to find companies to hire equipment from. So Jesus provided our own Iris rigs! Just this week I met with a top government official who told me that even the government was unable to find any company to drill wells in this desperate province of Cabo Delgado. The official was amazed and thrilled that our working rigs were actually in Pemba as we spoke.

Heidi: This dream, now being fulfilled, has been inside of me for years. I had a heavenly vision of our Iris teams going from village to village, drilling wells, planting crops and providing for the orphans, while preaching the Gospel through signs and wonders. Living Water flowing. We would then plant local mud hut churches every three miles or so, wherever there was the population to support them. We would train a number of Mozambicans per village in our Bible schools. They would receive the Father's heart and each care for from one to twelve orphans in their own villages. The wells would provide for the orphans' needs. I have had a vision to see Jesus care for *one million children* in my lifetime. Through God's power and provision, the well project will make this vision a reality.

The ball is rolling! I started by talking to four village chiefs about the well-drilling project and the idea of villagers trading small amounts of food for water, so that the orphans in the village could be fed. The village chiefs were thrilled by the idea. The local church loaded our Land Rover with sacrificial love offerings that included a goat, chickens, peanuts, cornmeal, tomatoes, peppers, sweet potatoes, coins, sifters, eggs, handmade ropes, sugarcane, potatoes and more. I wept as they laid such extravagant offerings at our feet. They wanted to provide for our orphan children in Pemba. This has been a truly beautiful day.

The journey of this project started long ago. After years of praying for drill rigs to bring water from the earth while we minister the Water of Life, on October 17, 2006, my assistant, Shara, and I flew to Denver, Colorado, for a prayer breakfast. We had a dear friend, Peter, who wanted me to preach to a small group of Christian businessmen.

Shara looked through my 2006 calendar and realized that there was only one free morning for the rest of the entire year, a small window in my schedule on Tuesday, October 17. Peter responded, "Perfect. The morning of Tuesday, October 17, is the exact time when a small group of business leaders meet to pray.". I shared the story of the Good Samaritan and Jesus stopping for the one. The Lord spoke to some of the business leaders and Bill Johnson and his family at Bethel Church about adopting this vision with us.

After two years of negotiating with the Mozambican government, bringing in an Indian well-drilling expert, paying duty, working through endless paperwork, finding a crane in Cabo Delgado big enough to lift the enormous rig, bringing in a well-drilling engineer from America and pressing through tremendous spiritual warfare, we have now officially broken ground. Even as I write we are drilling through solid rock!

Our church people pray for much fruit through this machine [drilling rig]

Auxiliary truck with water tank, pump and drill bits

Jesus is the Rock upon which He is building His Church in Mozambique. Rejoice with us as He answers His own invitation:

"*Come, all you who are thirsty*, come to the waters; and you who have no money, come, buy and eat! Come, buy wine and milk without money and without cost. . . . Give ear and come to me; hear me, that your soul may live. I will make an everlasting covenant with you, my faithful love promised to David."

Isaiah 55:1, 3 (emphasis added)

Miracles can happen on ordinary days. The Samaritan woman left her house on a day that started just like any other to fetch water from the nearby well. She was a woman who had been cast out, overlooked, forgotten, passed over. She was not a respectable church member or a pillar of society. Her name was more spat out than spoken.

I wonder if, as she walked to the well, she rummaged through the tangle of her broken life. Maybe she was trying to figure out how the tangle started. Maybe she had tried very hard, but things just kept breaking and all she had now was cracked and dry. She had cried herself out. Hers was a parched life.

So now she is at the water well. A man sits quietly. Not like any man she has met before, this man is Jesus, Son of the Living God. He asks her for a drink; she feels ashamed and inadequate. She is unprepared and unable. But He sees *beyond* her inability, He sees right into her soul, into the breaking and the dryness. He notices all the cracks. Jesus stops to notice *her*. He is committed, just to her. He talks gently about her life, but He sees her from a different point of view. His voice is all love.

Already the water is flowing over her parched life, her soul so used to going without, more accustomed to winter than to spring rain. She has nothing to offer, but *she is loved*, not inadequate, not unprepared or unable. Just loved. The bubbling, living grace water pours in over her cried-out dryness, washes over her shame and the years of stubborn dirt and stained memories. Now all she feels is different, clean, made whole. Even more than that, she feels ready.

This woman is loved and now she is different. She can go back to her village; she is ready for anything. She has power, because when you start to grasp how wide and long and high and deep is the love of Christ you start to get full of Him. With that fullness comes life bubbling over. So now on a day that started just like any other, nothing will ever be the same again.

Miracles happen on ordinary days, and just as Jesus brought dignity and eternal life to a Samaritan woman when He stopped and asked her for a drink of water from the well, He offers the same to you and me—*bubbling over life*—His gift to us, our gift to other parched lives. "The thief comes only to steal and kill and destroy; I have come that they may have life, and have it to the full" (John 10:10).

Is that not the best news ever?

Time to Reflect

Jesus answered, . . . "Whoever drinks the water I give him will never thirst. Indeed, the water I give him will become in him a spring of water welling up to eternal life." The woman said to him, "Sir, give me this water so that I won't get thirsty and have to keep coming here to draw water."

John 4:13–15

4

We Have Been Blessed

"Willing and longing."

Heidi: We have been blessed! And because God has blessed us we have been able to take in and educate even more beautiful children, reach more villages with the love of Jesus, drill more wells and train more pastors. We want to share some of these blessings from our Iris bases around the world. There is so much happening that we do not know how to share it all. Our heart's cry is for *even more* of Jesus' love and presence to be poured out among us.

During our Mozambican Christmas week, we were bouncing down a road, dust flying as we hit incredibly huge potholes, singing and praying with our Mozambican children in the truck. We were on our way to share the love and power of Jesus with a remote village.

Soon after our arrival, we performed our impromptu drama and preached a message. Before long, people were receiving Jesus as their Lord and Savior. I went around to the back of

We now have precious drinking water

the crowd with friends to pray for the blind and those too sick to make it to the front. After the first blind woman was healed, they started bringing more blind people to us. God healed them all! We will never grow tired of this!

After we returned home (and after much planning), a container arrived from Iris UK. We opened it to discover fabulous Christmas presents for all of our children at the Village of Joy in Pemba. There were wide smiles and eyes full of wonder as our children received their beautiful gifts, while their delighted house and missionary parents looked on. For our new treasures, this was the *first time* they had ever received a Christmas gift.

Harvest Bible College and Harvest School of Missions graduations were also a highlight for me. I sobbed as Rolland was awarded an Honorary Doctor of Ministry degree. All the students and children stood and cheered as Papa Rolland was honored in such a powerful and meaningful way. Dr. Don Kantel ended his speech with a charge to go "lower still." Students from all over Mozambique and twenty other nations laid their lives on the altar as they were commissioned to go *to the ends of the earth*, to carry the love of Jesus.

We had a powerful Holy Spirit baptism time in the turquoise Indian Ocean with Makua and Makonde converts willing and

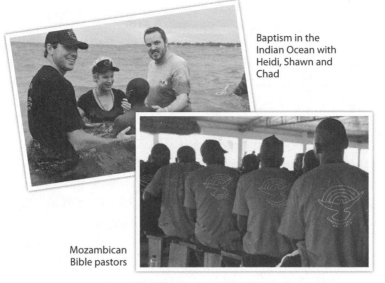

Baptism in the Indian Ocean with Heidi, Shawn and Chad

Mozambican Bible pastors

longing to die to their old lives and be resurrected to the new as they followed their Lord Jesus in baptism.

We have had a challenging year and alongside all of the joy have had some painful times as well. But we continue to press on toward the goal He has given us. We love Jesus more than life.

Here are just some of the things our Savior has been doing in our various Iris bases.

PEMBA BASE: DON KANTEL

Harvest, both spiritual and natural, is our year-round focus here at the Pemba Base and in our surrounding ministry centers. Our residential children's village in Mieze and our ministry into the whole Mieze community continue to be a source of much blessing. Our forty resident children in the "Village of Love" are now enjoying the fruit of their patience and labor in our farming projects. We currently have, for example, a fourth cycle of four hundred meat chickens almost ready for the table—a harvest that is eagerly anticipated by these young farmers for whom a chicken dinner is the best reward imaginable.

We have also been feeding and caring for eight laying hens that arrived as day-olds six months ago. Six months is an eternity in a culture where planning and working for the future is a rarity. But right on schedule, the first eggs appeared a couple of weeks ago. The kids were so excited! They could not wait to show them off. Several hundred eggs later, the children are still excited to retrieve every egg that is laid. They love hard-boiled eggs and are gradually being introduced to other egg dishes. Eggs for food are a rare luxury in rural Mozambique, and our children and staff are very thankful for the blessing of God they are experiencing through His bounteous harvest.

On our forty-acre Mieze farm we have more than fifty large mango trees laden with delicious fruit. This harvest will continue for about three months. A church in Ontario took a special offering to "buy" the yield from the farm so we can give it away instead of selling it. We are supplying mangos to hundreds of Mieze children through the church, as well as providing mangos for children at the Pemba Base and the adjacent Noviane Project.

We have just begun to divide the open farmland into half-acre plots so that church families can grow produce to eat and sell. A portion of what they harvest will be given back to the church for distribution to the poor and for use in the children's village. This "church co-op" will be an interesting farming experiment. We look forward to many kinds of harvests in the months ahead.

Then there is the spiritual harvest to celebrate. The Iris Pemba Base is surrounded by nearly fifty thousand poor villagers, almost all of another faith. One of our challenges over the past few years has been to develop effective ways of reaching villagers, especially children, with tangible expressions of the love of God. We have had various kinds of food programs, but have not been able to combine these very effectively with Christian content until recently.

Our Christian primary school has been our first successful, sustained effort. About 580 village kids attended this past year in addition to about 130 resident Iris kids. We had to turn some village children away due to overcrowding, so we have added three more classrooms for the new school year beginning in January.

During the past few months we have begun a daily program of Bible teaching, stories, games and hot meals for village kids at the Pemba Base. This is a high-energy program, conducted mostly in Makua, involving many staff and helpers each day for an hour and a half. We are now getting close to having six hundred children every day! Many have accepted the Lord, are praying and are even having visions of Jesus. More and more of these children are also now coming regularly to our Pemba church services, where we have also just begun to have a separate children's hour. Then we feed eight hundred or more children, plus hundreds of adults, every Sunday following church.

We have trained leaders from Mieze to run a similar village program there. This new program is now being attended by more than three hundred enthusiastic children. The first week we prepared rice and beans to serve an expected 150 children—yet more than three hundred received a full serving. God seems to like doing that for these precious Mieze kids!

Finally, after many months of planning and praying, it looks as though we may be about to acquire some property on Ibo Island to begin our next major project based on the Mieze model. This will be a challenging new initiative for many reasons and will require much prayer.

ZIMPETO BASE: STEVE AND ROS LAZAR

Everything is growing! Our baby house has been full to the brim, so we have now built a nursery for eight babies under six months old. Our Marracuene youth project continues to expand. There are now ten houses and 23 youths there, plus a blossoming church. Samaritan's Purse Ireland has helped us build a carpentry workshop. This will provide skills training and employment for several youths.

We are ministering to the orphans and widows, partnering with Iris Canada and Homes of Hope to build our first widows' house just above the property. This will house eight elderly women who will run our small farm and chicken project.

We were blessed to partner with the United States Embassy and Samaritan's Feet to give more than two thousand pairs of shoes to eight very poor communities. Every person received a foot washing, medical and dental attention, prayer and encouragement, as well as new shoes!

God continues to bless our reintegration program; about twenty children were reunited with their families in the last week. We continue to be challenged every day, but God is faithful and generous to us in all things.

LICHINGA BASE: THE WILCOX FAMILY

We have witnessed many answered prayers in our little corner of Mozambique. The locals consider the province of Niassa to be "the forgotten province." During the war it was the "Siberia" of Mozambique and the despised, disabled, unemployed and prostitutes were sent here.

Now Jesus is taking that which was despised and making it into something beautiful so that,

> "My name will be great among the nations, from the rising to the setting of the sun. In every place incense and pure offerings will be brought to my name, because my name will be great among the nations," says the LORD Almighty.
>
> Malachi 1:11

Missionaries, pastors and students at Lichinga

Meeting at our church in downtown Lichinga

God has given us two precious brothers, Victo and Anold, who have been visiting local villages. They told us this recent story of the power of Jesus at work.

Victo and Anold found themselves ministering to a deeply disturbed man and his family. The family was at a loss to know what to do for their nephew. Their solution was to tie him up and keep him in a little dark room to prevent him from beating others. He could not speak sensibly; all that came out of his mouth was nonsense. The witch doctors had been called for to begin applying their traditional medicines.

"But all this is not working!" the uncle explained to Victo and Anold. "My nephew just gets worse and worse."

Victo began to share the truth. "The evil spirits that are in the witch doctor make the man worse," he said. "Darkness will never flee from darkness! Only light causes darkness to flee."

49

When the family was faced with the challenge of choosing to believe either in God's power or in the witch doctor, they admitted they were too afraid to remove the traditional medicine that had been placed around the disturbed man's neck.

"No!" they said. "The madness that has come upon him could be transferred to us if we take off the necklace and burn it. It's better to call the witch doctor himself to come and remove it."

Anold and Victo said, "We believe that our God will never allow this madness to come upon us. He has power and He protects us. If you would like it, we can take off the necklace ourselves and burn it."

They agreed and the family watched these men of God, Africans like them, working in the authority of Jesus Christ, sure in the knowledge that the evil spirits the people here live in fear of had no power over them.

"And they saw that we were perfectly fine!" says Anold triumphantly. "We prayed for the mad man and encouraged the family that he would be well. Since that day, the Lord has been doing an amazing work in this young man's life. The family recognizes the work of God. Their nephew is recovering from all he went through, both physically and emotionally."

A week later, Peter Wilcox went to visit this man and was thrilled to see him in his right mind. Neither was he tied up anymore.

"You must arise," Peter told him. "You must make a decision in your heart and mind to overcome, because the Lord loves you very much and has a plan for your life. Do you understand?"

The man nodded. "I understand."

We praise Jesus for His awesome power and His liberating love! We continue to pray that after seeing God's hand in such a miraculous way, both the family and the young man will give their hearts to this Jesus who set him free. May all fear of what their neighbors might say be washed away by His grace.

Building a dorm for our new center in Lichinga, Niassa Province

MADAGASCAR BASE: CAROLINE THOMAS

At the end of last year God led me to the Iris Ministries Mission School. I learned so much and loved spending time with the children. During the last two weeks of school, God began speaking to me about my future. Heidi challenged us that if we were prepared to lay our lives down for Jesus, and if we felt that we had to answer His call to missions, to come forward and ask God to show us His plans.

I went up and as I began to pray I had a vision of a room of abandoned babies, lying in rags in the darkness. They were still, cold and silent. I began to cry and ask God to give me those babies. One by one the babies started to die—first one, then another—until they had all died. He then showed me one more vision of a baby being left in a Dumpster, abandoned at night in the dark. I cried and begged God, please, could I go to them and please, could they live and know that they were loved?

When I opened my eyes, my face soaked with tears, sitting right in front of me was a precious little Iris girl, only nine years old. She grabbed me and just held me. I heard God whisper that

51

she had been sent, right then, as a sign. I would get to hold the children so that they would live and know love—that just as I was holding her, I would hold them.

The next day Heidi was teaching again. At the end of class she said that if people had seen pictures of God's calling for them, and if they wanted God to show them a country and a city, to come up and ask Him. I was up at the front like a shot!

I asked God where the babies were and He said, *Madagascar*. I could hardly believe it since Madagascar is the country that I love, having previously spent six months there as a midwife. I felt as though God was saying to start an Iris base there, as this was the DNA of Iris—to save abandoned babies and let God restore them back to life.

I spoke with Heidi about it and she told me that she had been praying for someone to go to Madagascar for years. After speaking with her and some of the long-term staff at Iris, we decided to start Iris Madagascar with a baby house!

I booked a ticket to Madagascar on the way home from Mozambique, to visit my friends there and ask them all that I could about abandoned babies. They told me that babies were being abandoned in the capital and that they had heard stories of babies being abandoned in Dumpsters to die. Many of the orphanages were so full that there was a big need for a baby house there.

I am in the process of setting up the Iris Madagascar baby house—God's baby house where He can restore His precious babies back to life and they can know that they are loved. I am working on the paperwork to get Iris registered, praying in money and especially about building the right team, the team that God has chosen for this very special and exciting work!

CHIMOIO BASE: JENNIFER WENNINGKAMP

What a major blessing for the city of Chimoio! Since eight o'clock last night the skies have been filled with rain clouds.

We have longed for rain. Praise God that He heard so many simple prayers lifted by our Mozambican friends for their small crops that were beginning to wither in the African heat. Now we have joy and blessing to share. God has answered our prayers. We are one united body, all around the world!

Iris Sierra-Leone: Andrew Sesay

When I started the Beach Road Church, I was led to teach about the Holy Spirit. The people believed when I taught them how to pray for the sick to be healed and we now have many testimonies of how God has healed people in this young church.

One of our church members, Emmanuel, saw a young lady of another faith in serious pain from a chronic headache and asked if he could pray for her. While praying, he felt something moving from his hand, but nothing specific happened and he went on his way. Weeks later he saw the young lady again. She told him that after the prayer she had felt dizzy and gone to sleep. She had a dream that a man in a long white robe came and operated on her head, removing something. When she woke up there was no more pain. She was completely healed!

Iris Sudan: Michele Perry

We have grown! From 63 children to 84 on compound at Yei Children's Village. We have also adopted a second center on the border of Kenya with about ten more children.

We began an "In Community Care" program to care for orphaned children, within their extended family structures where possible, providing help with schooling and food. Some forty children are being cared for in this way.

Bricks of Hope has helped us to raise more than 60 percent of the needed funds for the initial development of our land. We have planted multiple churches and partner with several more churches in our newly formed Iris Sudan Revival Alliance, to disciple leaders and unite for prayer and intercession, joining our hearts and voices to see God's plans come to pass.

Our long-term missionary team is also growing! God has provided Jennie-Joy, a precious gal to be on my personal administrative team, and several more people are coming to serve here.

The Simple Message

Heidi: Despite what many would have us believe, the Gospel is not complicated. It is very simple. Jesus has given us everything we need. It is so simple that a child of three can get it: *Love God and love the one in front of you.* It is not about how to fill a building, build a reputation or make sure there is plenty of room to wiggle out of it all. It is just this: *Love God and love the one in front of you.*

I could tell you wild stories about church growth, food multiplying, blind eyes seeing, deaf ears popping open. But it all starts with the one person, one child; just like Jesus, stopping for the one. It is not about looking at ourselves, at our church, but looking right at Him. He has shown us how to *live* with passion, to *love* with compassion.

Never let anyone turn you away from understanding His heart. Do nothing to gain the approval of man, but in humility consider others better than yourself as you come to understand more and more why His love requires that *the first shall be last and the last shall be first.*

Often at church meetings we ask people to stand up if they want something. But if we are looking for apostles of His love, surely these people will not be standing up, they will be lying down! That is ministry: each of us looking not to our own interests, but rather to the interests of others. That is apostolic love—caring more about other people than yourself.

We are called to love our neighbor as we love ourselves. That means we cannot hate ourselves, because we do not want to duplicate that! So we need to understand how much God loves each one of us. God loves you as He finds you; He loves both who you are and also who you can become. He made each one of us to be who we are, just as children in the same family can be so different. He loves us even when we are stupid. And when we fall over, He will always pick us up and dust us off. He sees our hearts:

> "Then the righteous will answer him, 'Lord, when did we see you hungry and feed you, or thirsty and give you something to drink? When did we see you a stranger and invite you in, or needing clothes and clothe you? When did we see you sick or in prison and go to visit you?' The King will reply, 'I tell you the truth, whatever you did for one of the least brothers of mine, you did for me.'"

> Matthew 25:37–40

This is my prayer: God, open our eyes to Your love and compassion for the man, woman or child in front of us every day. For the one who has been kicked and spat on, who is broken, messed up and alone. For the rich man who is starving on the inside, the young boy who does not know when he will eat again, the girl in the dress that has been ripped to rags. Help us to preach in the street, to preach right in the dirt.

Jesus wants you and me to love Him first and wholly and then to love someone else. This is the Gospel, this is the price, this is our place and our purpose. This, beloved, is where *real* life and *real* joy are to be found!

Time to Reflect

"A new command I give you: Love one another. As I have loved you, so you must love one another. By this all men will know that you are my disciples, if you love one another."

John 13:34–35

PART 2

THE CUP OF JOY
AND SUFFERING

5

Unstoppable Love and a Boat

"He will make a way, where there is no way."

Rolland: We have just returned from ministering in some of the northern coastal villages of Mozambique. A man who had been unable to hear or speak was miraculously healed on the first evening. As always, it was a truly awesome experience. Everyone in the village knew this man, so the healing was greeted with widespread excitement, exuberant cheering and clapping. Now the whole village wants to follow Jesus!

We slept at the village and began our next day fresh at 4:30 a.m., when the whole village awakened. That morning we held a beautiful wedding at a church in a mud hut. The church family and all the local children sang and danced loudly in celebration of the couple's union. After that, we went to visit people in their homes and pray for the sick.

God continues to do glorious miracles among us. So many people were hungry for spiritual food that we might almost have forgotten how hungry they were for natural food, but after breakfast we saw ravenous children scraping out the bottoms of our pans after the pastors and visitors had eaten. The Lord again put it strongly on our hearts that *love looks like something.* So we prepared lunch and everyone in the village who was hungry ate. We left solar-powered audio Bibles and a soccer ball, and then we were on our way to another village.

Our next stop was a village where we had planted a church several years ago. The young, motivated pastor has been through two training sessions at Iris and is doing well. We will not stop until every village and tribe is reached by the unending, bottomless, ceaseless love of Jesus. His love compels us.

"Get a Boat!"

Heidi: The following story is really close to my heart. In part it is about the boat that took us on our outreach, but it is really about *tenacious love.*

One day Rolland was flying me in our little bush plane over a certain area of Mozambique when I noticed that there were no roads at all there. I asked Rolland to take me as low as the plane could possibly go, and when he did, I saw village after village passing below us.

I started sobbing! I was sobbing because there were no roads, so it seemed as if there would be no natural way for me to get to those people. I was weeping because I know my God, and I cannot imagine anyone on this planet not having the opportunity to know Jesus! I cannot imagine not doing everything I can to give them the chance. I wept and asked God what I should do and He said, *"Get a boat!"* So, we began to pray and we believed for a boat to somehow be provided.

For two years I was told again and again how impossible it is to get a boat to Pemba. Likewise, many of you reading this are chosen and called by God for great tasks, but there may be people telling you why you cannot go and why it is impossible for you to do what God is telling you. They may try to explain how impossible it is in great detail. They may quote books about what they think you cannot do and what they think God cannot do. I have read those kinds of books! But the Bible tells us what we *can do*. I know my God. If He says, *"Go and get a boat,"* He means that we should *really* go and get a boat.

So we got a boat!

Then the government said that we could not bring it into the country without paying the 70 percent import duty. God had provided, so I said, "Here is the money; give me the boat!" No one is going to stop me. Actually, I got really angry at the devil. How could he think he could possibly stop us? *When you are in love, you are unstoppable!*

It took two years and ten days for the boat finally to get here. On the way, while it was being hauled overland on rough roads, the transporters damaged the hull and put cracks in both the engines. At one point, the donors who had paid for the boat came to see us and it was still just sitting there, waiting for repairs, covered in dust and dirt in the backyard of a non-Christian man who owns most of the city. Their investment was not looking very impressive. I thought, *God, this is not what I had planned.*

Sometimes it is like this. It looks as though your vision is in the camp of someone who does not even know God. It looks as though your vision has been captured and carried away. It is full of dust, covered over and without any fuel. And yet God says, *"Believe what I said. And do not stop!"* Love is tenacious. Faith is tenacious. Love does not give up, even when the engines are toast and you have to pay 70 percent duty! Do not stop short of His promise to you. Do not stop short of your destiny. *Do not stop short of His glory.*

I had to keep searching for somebody to fix the boat, and even some of the people I love most told me repeatedly that it could not be done. Finally, I found a Filipino man who said he could repair it—but it took another year just to get the parts. After that, I was told that I would not be able to get close to those villages because the hull was too deep to travel up the shallow coastal waters. So I asked for a dinghy. I was told, once again, that this could not be done. For some reason we could not get a dinghy in Mozambique. But I was convinced that there surely must be a dinghy available somewhere. I had seen them! Someone said to me, "You just don't stop, do you?"

I cannot stop. Everybody needs to know—every tribe, every nation, every tongue. I am a woman possessed by His heart for the lost, wholly possessed by the One I love.

After another few months, we finally found a dinghy to go with our boat. The day we took the boat on our first outreach, one of the engines blew. But the other one worked! Of course, it would have been nicer to have two engines, but since we had one, I told the captain to keep going.

When we got to our first village, first by boat and then by dinghy, everyone who lived there came running to us and I was able to tell them that I had come with Good News.

I shared every word that I knew in their tribal tongue of Makua. They had never heard the name of Jesus before that day. We sat in a little carpenter's shop, which consisted of a few sticks and a ripped piece of plastic, and shared all about Jesus while some of the vil-

lagers made furniture. Everyone came. I shared, I sang and I gave them some little solar-powered audio New Testaments in Makua. When I asked them who wanted to receive Jesus, they all said yes!

What if we had stopped short?

What if we had given up?

Never stop short of your promise. Do not stop short of your destiny. Do not stop short of His glory.

A few months later we went back to this little village and even before I had the chance to get out of the dinghy, almost the whole village had run up to me, singing songs and quoting Scriptures they had memorized from their solar Bibles. What a joy! God has made Himself known to this village that had been totally forgotten by the outside world. We are now in the process of building a church and a school there, the first of either that the village has ever seen.

What a privilege we have, to share the Gospel about Christ Jesus! Oh, thank You, Jesus. We get to be part of bringing people into Your presence. We get to give our little lives. Without Jesus we are just dry twigs. But He calls us to fruitfulness, to intimacy and to *fearless, tenacious love*. Whatever it costs . . . we count it all joy.

Room to Grow

Jesus wants to live in us and He wants us to live completely in Him. He loves us so much that He will take a wrecking ball to our little houses and our tiny hearts. He wants His love to have room to grow in us *so much* that He will take our houses apart brick by brick to make more room. This is Christ *in you*, the hope of glory.

> Now I *rejoice* in what was suffered for you, and I fill up in my flesh what is still lacking in regard to Christ's afflictions, for the sake of his body, which is the church. I have become its servant by the commission God gave me to present to you the word of God in its fullness—the mystery that has been kept hidden for

ages and generations, but is now disclosed to the saints. To them God has chosen to make known among the Gentiles the glorious riches of this mystery, which is *Christ in you, the hope of glory.*

Colossians 1:24–27 (emphasis added)

Some people think that Paul was a grumpy man, but the evidence is right here: Paul was happy! Here he is talking to the Colossians and he is *rejoicing* in his suffering. He is happy to be suffering, overjoyed to be afflicted for the sake of Jesus, whom he loves more than life. Paul is readily drinking the Cup of Joy and Suffering.

What if Paul had stopped short? *What if he had given up?* Paul did not give up, and God did not give up on Paul.

God, who began to work in you before you were even born, before you knew how to say His name or even to pray, will not leave you finished or half-finished. He will *complete* the work that He set out to do in and through you. Never stop short of God's promise. Do not stop short of your destiny. Do not stop short of His glory.

The Holy Spirit will burn in your life and mine with tenacious and holy fire so that He can take us over. He wants us to be ready so that we can be full of Jesus, full of hope, full of nothing but God's glory being revealed to an empty and hopeless world. If you are empty, if you are broken, then He will fill you. If you know what it is like to be desperate, to be utterly needy, He will nourish and sustain you. And when you are full of Jesus, full of His hope and His glory, Christ *in you* will fill others just *like you.*

One unforgettable day, Jesus took a wrecking ball to my heart. He stood in front of me, in all the beauty of His presence, and held out a poor man's cup, a half-a-coconut cup. He asked me, "Heidi, this is the Cup of Suffering and Joy. Will you drink it?"

I drank and that cup became water for others. Jesus wants us to see as He sees. He looked into hell with heaven's laughing

65

eyes. He suffered. He was tortured and He died. He literally gave Himself away. He drank the Cup of Suffering and Joy; He suffered with *joy* set before Him.

You are not big enough, strong enough, prepared enough or spiritual enough to do the work that God wants you to do. But He is. God is more than big enough. He will complete the work He has set out to do in and through you. Never stop short of His glory, beloved.

Time to Reflect

God has chosen to make known among the Gentiles the glorious riches of this mystery, which is Christ in you, the hope of glory.

Colossians 1:27

6

News from Pemba

"His every word."

Brian and Lorena Wood: Jesus has shown Heidi that *love looks like something*. At our Pemba base we began to feed lunch daily to children from the surrounding villages. These children come from very poor families, and in this culture's pecking order they are always last. But the children are hungry in more ways than one.

When we arrived at Pemba base in June 2008, we started teaching Bible lessons to the children every day as they waited for their food: "Man does not live on bread alone, but on every word that comes from the mouth of God" (Matthew 4:4).

With help from Harvest Bible College students we have been able to run our Bible program five days a week and have seen incredible growth in these precious children. We now have eight hundred children learning with us. Just this week a new building was dedicated for use in the program, as well as for teaching God's Word to the Iris Elementary School children. Our

Mozambican co-worker, Elder, has named the building, which is positioned at the top of a hill, "Mount Sinai." He says, "The Word of God is emphasized each day here, just as God gave His commands to Moses, and Moses passed them on to the children of Israel. Likewise we pass on God's Word."

God has gifted Elder tremendously and we feel privileged to work with him. He hopes to attend the internship program with Metro Ministries soon and envisions training many leaders for children's ministry in the future.

I asked Elder, "What is the best thing you've seen come out of the Bible study program?"

He answered, "Children coming to know the true God and seeing their lives change. Before, the children who came for lunch each day showed no respect, no love and no obedience. Now we all see a change in them. They know the love of Jesus, they sing, they talk about Him, how *He is the way, the truth and the life*. It's fun to be with the children. I love seeing the peace and joy in their faces. I know that with God's help they will help to transform the villages where they live."

We trust and pray that God's Word and His Spirit will continue to grow *mightily* in our children. Here is a testimony from one of our precious girls, Tufa, translated from Makua:

Hello, my name is Tufa. I'm ten years old and I have been attending this program for about seven months. I'm thankful to God for His love and for bringing me here, where I can learn more about Him and the Bible. I'm thankful because *He is changing my heart*. Here I have learned how to talk to God. I used to be tormented by evil spirits in my room every night; I couldn't sleep. But then I learned about God here and I started to pray. Now the spirits don't come anymore. My parents are happy that I'm not afraid to go into my room. Recently, I lost my school uniform blouse. I started to pray. When I went back to the school, I found it! I'm thankful to God for His love. He answers my prayers.

I asked Tufa to tell me the most important thing she has learned here. She said, "To listen to the Word of God and follow it." I was so excited to hear this!

We consider it such an honor to be here and to minister to these dear ones. Every story and lesson is brand new to them. What they hear is received with eager, hungry hearts as they learn more about their heavenly Father each day.

Heidi: I want to finish well. I do not want to end up burned out, tired out and dead in the water. Paul finished well: "In all my prayers for all of you, I always pray with joy because of your partnership in the gospel from the first day until now" (Philippians 1:4–5). He carried on doing what God told him to do and here he is again, happy! He is a happy man.

He is happy because he knows that he is not alone. God is working on Paul's behalf. God is working *in* Paul; all Paul has to do is work *with* God. It is a glorious partnership like no other. God and me. God and you. That is unstoppable love. God is not going to leave us to figure it out all by ourselves. He is not going to leave us out on a limb. God is with us and He is for us: Christ *in you* the hope of glory.

We live by the ocean in Cabo Delgado, and I enjoy walking up and down the beach. I like to talk with God there. Quite often I watch a group of men or women casting a big net into the waters, about twenty men or twenty women, depending on what kind of net they are using. They sing together as they pull in the fish—sing and pull, sing and pull.

There is no way that one person could pull in one of those heavy nets on his own. So they work together, happy; sing and pull, sing and pull. God showed us how to work in partnership by demonstrating how the Father, Son and Holy Spirit work *together*; never alone, always preferring each other, esteeming each other.

That is what makes the work a joy—*partnership*. We have children as young as six praying for those in need, praying for deaf ears and blind eyes to open. They pray and the ears and eyes open. These children do not have three years of theological training, they just know that God offers equal employment opportunities; work for all. We cannot do it alone, we have to release our sons and daughters, root for them, encourage them and believe that they can do more than we can, always preferring each other.

You cannot do something that is God's work when you are isolated and vulnerable—any more than I could attempt to cook for fifty thousand people on my own. You may have enough strength to catch one big marlin fish and stand there holding it, but your arms are going to get tired and soon you will not have enough energy for the full harvest. We have to both support and *release* one other—to worship, to minster, to harvest, to build—each doing the good work that he or she was created to do. If we support and release each other, we will not end up so exhausted.

We will be desperate and frustrated if we try to do everything on our own, because our strength will fail. We want to give ourselves away, to release the gifts and talents of those around us so that they can go further and faster than we can. We take great comfort and joy in doing God's work together.

Do what God has given you to do, do it with joy and do it *together*. God and me. God and you. That is unstoppable love!

Time to Reflect

I always pray with joy because of your partnership . . .
being confident of this, that he who began a good work in
you will carry it on to completion until the day of Christ
Jesus.

Philippians 1:4–6

7

Simple, Practical Love

"Love looks like something."

Heidi: Last Thursday, in true Iris fashion, teams of mission school students, Bible college students, missionaries and visitors poured into a small flock of Land Rovers, venturing out into the Mozambican bush to wreak havoc on the enemy and see the Kingdom of God advance.

In the district of Chiúre, God healed many of the sick on the first night, including three deaf people who had their ears opened up. God's presence fell heavily during the worship service the next morning, and afterward we walked through the village to the local watering hole for an incredible time of baptism. Throughout our stay, our Makua and Iris team members remained full of joy and energy. Before we left, the local Muslim family who had allowed us to camp on their land accepted Jesus also.

Of course, it seems that none of our trips is without certain amusing difficulties. On this trip we lacked the large open-backed truck that we normally use for a stage. Without it, our Bible college and Bible school students struggled gamely through a prepared drama, without any of the usual boundaries to the play's action. The effect was hilariously chaotic as the crowds

intermingled closely with our actors. The sound system had to be cranked up to amplify the voices of the actors over those of the close-up audience. The result was loud and messy, but nonetheless *beautiful*.

We received a very generous offering from this village—a fully grown live goat, who provided ample sound effects of his own as he rode proudly on top of our Land Rover down the dusty road to home. We are glad to say that he is now safely settled with an ever-growing family of fellow goats at our Mieze children's home.

One of the most moving parts of our trip was when a Makua grandmother brought us a beautiful albino orphan named Mariette. Albino children are difficult to care for in the villages as their skin and eyes require special protection in the hot, sunny, subtropical climate. We are now working with officials there to bring this precious baby to Pemba. There is great need for a new children's home in Chiúre, as there are 48 orphans in the one village we visited alone. We are in the process of building a hut there, and we continue to believe God for *His increasing provision* as we take in every orphan we can find, both here and from all over the country.

Everyday Love

Love looks like something. It finds its expression in numerous, creative ways. Four years ago in southern Mozambique, one of our African youths shared his dream to see Mozambican worship music change the world. At the time, no resources were available for this music to be distributed, but his vision persisted.

Last year, that same young man was part of a pilot project in Pemba. Armed with generously funded new recording equipment, he recorded a full-length album of beautiful Makua songs called *Voice of the One*. We hope the songs will influence the culture here and abroad for the Kingdom, and that they will prove to be the first fruits of far more indigenous and heavenly art to come.

What does love look like for a widow in an old house? Our friend Edward Palma says, "We wanted to demonstrate the love of the Father to the oldest and poorest widows in a very tangible way. And here and now, *love looks like a new roof* before the rainy season.

"Helped by some of our local Mozambican Bible students and pastors, our team arrived to fix one roof so full of rifts and ruptures that it could not really be described as a shelter. As we tore the old covering off, it crumbled in our hands, brittle from years of sun and rain. Several generations of women were living in the house. The eldest celebrated with a bright, toothless smile.

"The project soon attracted many neighborhood children so we split our team, half of us in the dirt dancing and playing with the kids. One of the Makua widows and I taught the children a song, proclaiming that no matter where you look *you won't find anyone like Jesus.* And to top it all off, just a few dollars bought bread for all the children.

"The message of the Gospel is clear: Love is not just an ideal, it is action; love in reality, in spirit and in truth. How good it is to be with the poor and to pour out simple, practical love! We will continue to repair roofs as often as funds allow."

Jamie Human writes, "Yesterday we celebrated birthdays for all of our children born in July. For each of our children a birthday is more than just a fun day; it is a reminder that they are *adopted into a family*. They are no longer orphans who do not have names or birthdays. We want each of them to feel a special and renewed sense of belonging at these festivities.

"The celebration was held on the serene Wimbe Beach, and the children had an incredible time. One of our missionaries, Yonnie, is in charge of the *ministry of fun*—a great priority here at Iris. She had the kids split into teams, and we held relay races up and down the beach. Though competing in teams, everyone was just happy to be out having fun, with no concept of prize-winning. After team *Alegria* won the last relay, all of the kids from the different teams erupted into dancing and singing. They are so grateful to be a family, having fun, that there is no jealousy.

"When it came time to pass out the gifts, everyone began praising and thanking God and, of course, dancing! Each child who had a birthday was called into the circle and given a gift bag with toys and a new outfit. Some of the children and missionaries prayed a prayer of blessing over the children as they received their gifts. Afterward we all dined eagerly on much-prized cake. Anything sweet is a highly anticipated treat in Pemba.

"The children look forward to these celebrations once a month. They are *so thankful for God's provision*—to be adopted and surrounded by people who love and support them. What a blessing to celebrate this way!"

A Day in Our Lives

We went on another perfectly normal outreach last night. Which is to say, most of the villagers gave their lives to the Lord on the first night, and one young boy who had been deaf received his hearing. We fell asleep happy in our little circle of tents.

The next day began at three a.m. when the children sleeping in the nearest mud-walled hut scrambled to sweep up the dirt around our tents and peer through our netting. I looked up to see stars shooting across the incredible African sky—our own billion-star hotel! I thanked Jesus for the *privilege* of being in such a hungry place and started boiling water for that most happy and comforting of all bush drinks: Starbucks coffee.

After serving about fifty of our friends, I had the joy of leading the police who had guarded our tents and vehicles on this outreach to the Lord. They prayed with their AK-47s still slung over their shoulders. This is known as a dangerous area and the last time we were here many of our things were stolen. I lost my phone, camera, passport and extra clothes. My documents and clothes were eventually returned after one of our oldest boys decided to pursue the bandits through the night, though on that occasion the clothes came back with a bullet in them!

After praying with the police, we visited Marietta, in the district of Mecúfi, to attend a double wedding. The local mud hut church was too small for all the guests, so we went out under a beautiful, giant shade tree for the ceremony. The two couples sat on a grass mat and all the local villagers worshiped with our pastors in celebration. We were hugely blessed to be able to place gold wedding rings in each of these couples' hands. One of the couples had a newborn baby, five days old, and we dedicated her to the Lord Jesus. Then we began a joyful walk to a nearby river so that we could baptize all the new believers who had joined us.

On the way we came across a five-year-old girl called Joanna. Joanna had never walked in her life, and her knees were crusted over with calluses from years of crawling in the dirt. I felt the Father's compassion for her, so I picked her up by her two hands and called her to walk. I steadied her spindly legs and blessed her to come. Many of us cried when she did come, walking for the first time. What a joy! Imagine: We get to be alive for such a time as this.

Later we walked for several kilometers, passing through another charming village filled with friendly greetings. We were joined by so many more people that we soon became a parade of hundreds. When we finally reached the river, breathtakingly beautiful as it flowed into a lagoon just before the Indian Ocean, we began to baptize people. Many of those we baptized came out of the water praying in tongues, with the Holy Spirit very much present. The joy never ends! During the baptisms, little boys were doing backflips on the shore.

Afterward, my daughter, Crystalyn, and I went swimming with a little flock of children close behind. We noticed from their stickers that these boys had been in our children's service that morning, so we asked them if they, too, wanted to follow Jesus forever. Six more young lives followed the Lord Jesus in baptism.

After a long walk back to our vehicles and a quick plate of beans and rice for lunch, we raced back up the rough dirt roads to Pemba for our monthly Iris birthday party. It is always such a thrill to be able to look each one of our children in the eye and speak to them about the glorious and special destiny that the Father has planned for them. Each one receives a gift, a lot of prayer and some of our homemade cake. Some of our girls stay up all night, happily cooking for this occasion. Every month we so look forward to this wonderful day.

After a round of meetings to discuss some of our upcoming new programs for individual child sponsorship and combating poverty, three of the older boys, who have been with us at Iris since they were small children and are now leaders in our ministry, surprised us with a fish dinner. They had made the fabulous meal themselves, with *great love*. I do believe I have just had the perfect day. All praise to the Father, great things He has done.

To live is Christ, to die is gain. We have to let go of our preconceived ideas, our carefully worked-out plans, our way of doing things, so that God can live in us. We need new life, His life. If we are going to make room to carry His glory, then we have to die first. We have to take our places at the cross and say, as Jesus said, "Not My will but Yours, God, Your will. I will drink the Cup You have called Me to drink, whatever the cost."

Time to Reflect

And this is my prayer: that your love may abound more and more in knowledge and depth of insight, so that you may be able to discern what is best and may be pure and blameless until the day of Christ, filled with the fruit of righteousness that comes through Jesus Christ—to the glory and praise of God.

Philippians 1:9–11

8

Finish Your Assignment

"Not my will, but Yours be done."

Heidi: When the worst cyclone to strike Mozambique in many years hit in 2000, I was on a boat. It was not the little boat that we use to reach the villages in the country that cannot be reached any other way. I was on a comfortable boat filled with friends, great food and kindness.

I started getting phone calls from my sons. Everyone was in trauma. We had lost 360 churches—just wiped out by the floodwaters. I was on a nice boat, but *did not* want to be on that boat. My people were suffering and I wanted to go to them so badly I would have flown right there if I had had wings.

I did not have wings, but I do have Rolland, and he has his techie gadgets, so I begged him, "Get me off this boat, we have to go home. Please get us home!"

Rolland was doing his best to find us a way home despite the ravages of the cyclone, but meanwhile I was *stuck*. What do you do when you are stuck? You can flail your fists at the wind, cry and get more and more agitated, but all that happens is you become like a fly caught on a spider's web: The more you struggle, the worse you get stuck.

Paul wrote, "This is my prayer: that your love may abound more and more in knowledge and depth of insight, so that you may be able to discern what is *best*" (Philippians 1:9–11, emphasis added). What is best? When you are stuck the best thing you can do is to ask your loving Father, *What is best?*

Jesus said, "I only do what I see the Father doing." There is no point trying to get off a boat if you are meant to be on it. What if the very thing you are stuck in is His will? Well, then you drink the Cup of Suffering and Joy, finding joy in doing what you are meant to be doing—even if you have a "better" idea of where you should be and what you should be doing!

In Mozambique tens of thousands of people were being displaced and losing their homes. "Why can't I go home, God?" I protested. "I want to be with my sons and daughters!"

This is what He said to me: *Finish your assignment, Heidi. Release your sons and daughters. Let them loose. You have raised them well; now release them.*

Letting Go

When I know what God wants, then I can do it. I can relax and get out of the way. So I stayed on the boat. Do you know who got the trucks out? Who led the relief effort? One of our sons. Previously he had been a bandit, until one day when we found him by the side of the road with a knife in his hand and he said to us, "You have to take me with you."

He has been with us ever since. Release your sons and daughters. Give them the keys to your truck. Yes, they may crash the truck or forget to put oil in it, but how does anyone learn to be responsible without having some responsibility and making mistakes just as we did?

God told me to finish the assignment He had given me, to stay on the boat. Do not get in the way of God's glory. Do not stop short. Fix your eyes on Him. Trust His love. He is always more than enough. I pray that your love may abound more and more so that you will know God, you will be able to discern what is best, you will know in your heart what He wants you to do and you will trust Him to do what *only He* can do.

Under Fire

Some people think we made this next part up. Why anyone would make up something like this, I do not know. In fact, what happened was beyond imagination. I learned more about the Cup of Joy and Suffering during this time than ever before.

After the cyclone devastated Mozambique, I stayed faithful to the schedule that God had planned for me. I stayed on the boat as God told me. Then I left the boat when God told me to go and preach at Oxford University. Next I was due to speak at a historic meeting in a cathedral in France.

But then, back in Mozambique, half a mile or so away from one of our main bases at Zimpeto near Maputo, twenty tons of ammunition started to explode.

The heat had triggered one missile that acted as a catalyst for more explosions. Our son Norberto called us while the missiles were exploding; he had narrowly missed being hit by shrapnel. Two missiles had already hit the center, the altar of the church and the administration block.

"Mama, what shall we do?" Norberto sobbed. If I could have crawled through the phone line I would have, but I was thousands of miles away. "Pray for Father to shelter you and the children," I said. He was terrified. I prayed like a mother tiger, and we called my travel agent. "Please change my ticket," I begged. "I have to go home." And we kept on praying, and people kept on saying the same thing that God was saying to me: "Heidi, I think God is saying that you should finish your assignment."

Come on, Lord! You cannot possibly mean for me to visit a cathedral while bombs are going off and our children are terrified? The contact person at the cathedral called and said that I should definitely come, that it would be packed with monks and nuns and the church had not been that full for hundreds of years. *Finish your assignment!* So we called my travel agent back, "Very sorry. Please, can you change my ticket back again?"

Back at our base in Zimpeto, people were dying in the surrounding areas; the hospitals were taking in dozens of badly injured people. Fires were alight in our children's center. But Pastor Jose and Norbeto had rounded up the frightened children and they were in what was left of the church praying, worshiping.

> Whoever dwells in the shelter of the Most High will rest in the shadow of the Almighty. I will say of the LORD, "He is my refuge and my fortress, my God, in whom I trust." . . . He will cover you with his feathers, and *under his wings you will find refuge*; his faithfulness will be your shield and rampart. You will not fear the terror of night, nor the arrow that flies by day.
>
> Psalm 91:1–2, 4–5 (emphasis added)

No one was hurt. Not *one person* at the children's center was hurt. The Lord sheltered them under His wings. Our missionaries did not flee for their own safety. They all stayed to protect the children.

Meanwhile, I preached at the cathedral and the Holy Spirit met those starving monks and nuns with His compassion, encouragement, mercy, healing and joy. Starving people do not always look as though they are starving—they may be studying at Oxford

University or they may live in a monastery—but God sees and God knows. And if we will let Him, He will show us not just what He sees but *how* He sees.

When Rolland and I finally got back to Zimpeto we hugged our children. We could have expected that people would have scattered, but no one had left. No one had left when the floods came or when the name-calling, beatings, rock throwing and imprisonment happened—so they were not about to leave now.

So we held the most beautiful worship service I have ever been in. God had saved our children's lives and we were *thanking* Him for our very lives. Then we went out and ministered to the families around the base who had lost their homes and their lives. We took in three orphans who had lost their father to tuberculosis and now their mother to the missiles. We looked into the eyes of a mother who had lost her child and we drank the Cup of Joy and Suffering.

God says to you today, "Finish your assignment." However much you think you should be somewhere else, and however bad it gets, even if you have to live on the edge when everything in you is telling you to run to safety, *finish*. He, who began a good work in you and through you, will be faithful.

Fruitful Labor

In the days and weeks that followed the cyclone, the government said that the only way Iris Ministries could get involved in the relief effort was if we agreed to feed all of the people in all of the refugee camps—six thousand in one camp, six thousand in another, and so on.

The children in those camps were so hungry that they were not even crying anymore. They were silently sitting or lying in the dirt with their bloated stomachs and their mothers dying all around. What do you do? Do you look away and resign yourself to the inevitable? Do you listen to the little voice that tells you why it would be impossible to feed that many people?

"I pray that I may have sufficient courage," said Paul.

Sufficient courage to look right into the storm and the famine, to look right there at all the suffering and see heaven's provision. Enough courage to drink the Cup you are called to drink. This was suffering on a different scale altogether. Nothing can prepare you for it.

Do you trust Me, Heidi?

From screaming, *"Nooo!,"* I was learning to scream, "Yes, Lord! Yes, I believe we can feed these babies that do not have the strength to even cry anymore. You gave Yourself away. You gave everything You had and it is always more than enough."

During this crisis, in one week, we were given as many containers of food as in the last twelve years combined. We fed twelve thousand people a day, and then we fed more. The trucks rolled out, and the people were fed.

The Cup of Joy and Suffering. Seeing what God sees, something impossible, something you cannot begin to understand, something you want to fix. But if you try to fix it on your own, you will just burn out and die of exhaustion. So why not drink

86

the Cup and leave your impossible burden to Jesus? Not my will, but Yours be done, Lord.

It takes courage to go, but it can take more courage to *let go*. Let go of your way, let go of being the answer. You and I are not the answer, my friend, God is. If we live like this, if we will let go of the reins we think we have to hold on to, if we will trust Him as we finish our assignments, it will mean *fruitful labor*. If there is no fruit, what would be the point of living anyway? But the seed has to be buried deep in the ground before the fruit has a chance to take hold. Before the harvest is ready the fields look bare. All the life is hidden, ready to be revealed, ready to be released—in *His* time.

Time to Reflect

I eagerly expect and hope that I will in no way be ashamed, but will have sufficient courage so that now as always Christ will be exalted in my body, whether by life or by death. For to me, to live is Christ and to die is gain. If I am to go on living in the body, this will mean fruitful labor for me.

Philippians 1:20–22

9

Going Lower Still

"God gives the victory."

Rolland: As you may know, one of Iris Ministries' core values is *going lower still*. We feel that this applies in the natural as well as the spiritual and, over the last few months, we have certainly been going lower still in the well-drilling department! We have had many trials, but every one of them has worked together for good and the glory of God.

The most amazing news is that we have been issued a national government permit to drill wells anywhere in Mozambique. Although this may seem like a formality, in reality it is an outright miracle. Many organizations work for years to obtain a permit like this. But because of God's favor—with the tireless work of Iris's government relations manager, Serjio Mondlhane—we received our permit just a few weeks into the application process.

Getting the best people into the right roles is key to the success of any project, so we were so blessed that Iris missionary

Joe Vaine agreed to run the well-drilling project. Joe has experience in water management in other parts of the world, as well as serving as Iris's airplane pilot for the past couple of years. Joe has been busy interviewing people from all over—flying them in, bussing them in or calling them in from across town. They have come from southern Mozambique, Malawi, India and the United States.

Our team now consists of an extremely talented master driller from Malawi, plus a gentleman from the company that supplied our rigs in India and American, Jeff Johnson, who has missions-

development experience all over Africa, including well-drilling experience in Mozambique. Just as important, we will be training a small team of Mozambicans who will eventually take this program to another level. Joe has been drilling practice wells on our Iris base so that he and potential employees can get hands-on experience, working out all the mechanical kinks along the way.

Ribbon-cutting ceremonies are the order of the day. We will begin drilling our next well soon in the local village of Impiri, a village of 8,600 people. Impiri does not have a single well; the local people have to walk for miles every day to get water. After we have drilled two wells there, we will move on to Nacaramo, a village of more than four thousand people with no well.

These wells are the exciting culmination of a dream that Heidi has carried for years. The wells that we drill will become natural gathering places for our local communities, focal points for sharing the Gospel and the love of God. We rejoice together with these villages and all of heaven at this wonderful news.

Refreshing Waters

Meanwhile, great things continue to happen at our Iris base in South Africa. God is working on many fronts to accomplish His purposes.

Our friends Jean and Teisa Nicole write: "We are thrilled to announce the opening of Michaels Children's Village in Mbonisweni, South Africa. This dream began four years ago in the heart of our international director of Iris Ministries, Pastor Surprise Sithole. Mbonisweni is a poor township outside of Nelspruit, and after planting a church there, Surprise and his wife, Tryphina, soon discovered the vital need for a children's center to help the distressing number of orphaned, abandoned and abused children within the community.

"Prayer warriors at the local church and worldwide began to ask God to establish a thriving children's center. In 2008, Iris Ministries secured funding through supporters of Iris in America, the United Kingdom and Korea, and the property for the children's village was purchased.

"On July 25, 2009, Surprise's vision finally became a reality. We had a precious celebration service attended by more than two hundred people and leaders from the local community. We were so blessed as the first two houses were prayerfully dedicated to God, while our new house parents led the ribbon-cutting ceremonies. This is only the beginning. Many, many more homes will be opened in the future and our new baby house should open in the next two months.

"South African Social Services is currently in the process of placing the first round of children in our care. We are so thankful to God, who gives us this victory through our Lord Jesus Christ."

So we see signs of the Water of Life springing up everywhere. As we commit ourselves to go lower still—for less of us and more of Christ to be evident in our lives in increasing measure—He touches people and brings refreshment to the parched deserts of their lives.

Time to Reflect

Therefore, my dear brothers and sisters, stand firm. Let nothing move you. Always give yourselves fully to the work of the Lord, because you know that your labor in the Lord is not in vain.

1 Corinthians 15:58

10

In His Power

"We need Him."

Rolland: Heidi and I would both be dead by now if our doctors were to be believed. A few years ago Heidi was in the hospital for a month with an out-of-control staph infection. The doctors gave up and told her she could write her tombstone's epitaph. Then, suddenly, while she was preaching and in a lot of pain, God healed her. The next morning she was out jogging!

Four months ago I was diagnosed with terminal dementia. I was barely alive. I needed help to shower, change my clothes and clip my fingernails. I did not know what country I was in and could not remember anything from one day to the next. Heidi built a room for a full-time caregiver to look after me. The doctors said I did not have long to live and family was called to my side.

Despite all of this bad news, some faithful friends sent me to a Christian center in Germany where I received incredible medical care in a faith-filled environment. Today I am back in Pemba ministering the Gospel, ready to fly my plane again and reconnecting with our friends and staff. I look forward to pushing back the frontiers of missions in Sudan, the DR Congo (Democratic Republic of the Congo) and wherever God tells me to go.

We cannot function in this world without the power of the living God. Some of us have not yet been brought to our limits and are not yet fully aware of our complete dependence on Him. *But our time will come.* We need Him in order to stay alive. We need Him for our health. We need Him for our healing. We need Him for righteousness, peace and joy in the Holy Spirit.

We need Him more than talk. We need Him more than church, a missions program or financial support. We need more Him more than anything any human being can do for us. We need sheer, raw power poured into our lives through the goodness and love of God. We need power to appreciate God, to make Him the greatest pleasure in our lives. We need power to rejoice with joy inexpressible and full of glory. We need power to experience His Kingdom and to fulfill His purposes.

How does this power come to us? It is the *grace* and gift of God. He plants in us a hunger that will not be denied. He opens our eyes to our lack, to the poverty of living without His powerful Presence. He grants faith where there is none.

In His power we can rest even while under demonic attack. His power fixes our eyes on Him. In His power we are able to discipline ourselves in everything. We can cast our cares on Him because He is willing to use His power on our behalf.

How can we be sure He cares for us? We have only to look to the cross. We go to the cross, and there we find confidence to approach Him. The cross is never empty of its power. There and only there we find salvation of every kind. *At the cross* we come to know our God and His heart toward us. At the cross we learn to become utterly dependent on His power.

His Power in the Bush

Today we are driving to a village for outreach, the joy of our lives in Mozambique. The road is dark. Traffic is occasional. Our Land Rover is loaded on top with tents, sleeping bags—everything we need to stay overnight. We are carrying as many people as we can.

Along the way we explain to our visitors how we operate, planting churches every few miles along the roads. In seven years we have planted more than a thousand churches among the Makua alone, an "unreached and unreachable" people group in our Cabo Delgado Province. Today we are returning to a village we have visited before. Many people there know our worship songs.

Our advance team has already arrived and has set up a generator, sound system and video projector. As we approach our destination, the inky darkness is punctuated by bright lights, a screen and a whole village of people gathered together. As we draw closer we see that many people have come from neighboring villages.

Two languages are needed because of the diversity of the crowd: Portuguese and Makua. Heidi preaches and many are added to the faith. We pray for the sick and two deaf people are healed. The people sing and dance their hearts out. Clouds of dust rise in the floodlights as they express the joy of their salvation. *Heaven is touching down* in this remote spot on the planet as God visits the people of His choice. The power of God is transforming hearts and giving *hope*. The Kingdom of God is advancing yet again.

It is late now and our Makua team has prepared a feast for us: spaghetti! We each take a plastic plate from a stack and dip into a happy pot of plain spaghetti that we eat with our fingers. Village children come streaming in to eat with us. There are no latrines in the village, so we fend for ourselves in the sticks and bush. We manage to put up our tents with a few flashlights. Since we do this so frequently, Heidi and I bring cots. With no city lights to disturb them, the stars are magnificently and densely spread across the sky, the southern constellations so exotic to those of us from the Northern hemisphere.

We change into shorts to beat the heat of the night and squeeze into our tents, drifting off to sleep as we pray. The village is up and ready to go at daybreak. Heidi makes coffee for our team, and our Mozambican friends enjoy the experience of drinking this new treat. We have a service in the reed-and-mud church and, later, weddings to perform! Our visiting friend, Terry, speaks to the couples. Again the villagers erupt with singing and dancing. The joy is infectious.

The village is building a new church structure, but the people are almost penniless. We give them enough money to buy roofing materials, as they have already built the walls. They are thrilled. Our Mozambican team teaches AIDS awareness and gives a Bible study. We bless the people with final words of teaching and encouragement and leave the village amid a laughing, running crowd of children. We will be back!

The framework of a new church building coming together

On the way home we reflect with our visitors on what we are witnessing. There does not seem to be any limit to the number of churches we can plant if we have enough provisions and people to help. The whole province is coming alive. Everywhere the poor are welcoming the Good News and running to Jesus. We are just beginning to see what is possible in the Lord. *The best is always yet to be.*

Seeing As He Sees

Heidi: I was in church in Brazil, and I was on the floor as God showed me picture after picture of starving people crying out for food so that they could live and not die. Meanwhile, these same people were receiving from the Holy Spirit and they were laughing. "Are you schizophrenic, Lord?" I asked. But then He released me from the Cup of Suffering and I began to laugh, too. Now who looked schizophrenic!

But that is how He sees. He sees heaven right through hell. He sees freedom beyond the cross, He sees eternal life beyond the grave, and He sees laughter through the tears. People often ask me, How do you cook for all those children? Me, cook? You can ask Rolland: I could burn water. If I am cooking in our house there is always smoke. But God sends help. I do not do everything. I *cannot* do everything.

Philippians 2:5–8 says:

> Each of you should look not only to our own interests, but also to the interests of others. Your attitude should be the same as that of Christ Jesus: Who, being in very nature God, did not consider equality with God something to be grasped [used to His own advantage], but *making himself nothing*, taking the very nature of a servant, being made in human likeness. And being found in appearance as a man, he humbled himself and became obedient to death—even death on a cross!
>
> (emphasis added)

Here He is, the King of glory. He can stay anywhere, go anywhere, do anything. He knows who He is. And yet what does

He do—for us and for our sake? He empties Himself until He becomes nothing. The King of glory, Jesus, allowed Himself to be born in a borrowed stable with goats and chickens. He had to learn a language. He had to be clothed and fed by someone. He just gave Himself away, always preferring others. He left His Kingdom, left His glory behind to show us how to live.

While we are trying to hold on tight, He is saying, *Give it away.* He is equal with God in every way, but He made Himself nothing. He humbled Himself, and He was obedient to death. What a Teacher! All we have to do is follow the leader, be in unity with Him, see what He sees, go where He goes, do what He does, pray what He prays, love as He loves.

When we live like this, we will see every disaster with different eyes, "having the mind of Christ." We will see heaven right through hell, freedom through the cross, eternal life beyond the grave and laughter through the tears. God is big enough. We do not have to hold on so tightly; we can give ourselves away because Christ lives in us. *Christ in you, the hope of glory.* He is more than enough.

We carry His glory and His power and we humble ourselves, always preferring others. We see with the eyes of Christ, the eyes of faith. We see past what *is* to what *will be*. And we pray what He prays, go where He goes, loves as He loves. This way we will know life and life in all its fullness.

Time to Reflect

For it is God who works in you to will and to act according [in order to fulfill] his good purpose.

Philippians 2:13

11

The Spreading Kingdom

"Go, go, go!"

Rolland: From our boat deck, I looked past the short stretch of beach to a collection of stick-and-mud huts set back from the sparkling ocean on a small hill. This is the village of Londo, isolated by the wild bush and accessible only by sea. Until we landed here, the people of Londo had lived for generations without ever hearing the name of Jesus. But on learning of His love and power, they opened their hearts without reservation and now He is transforming this village, measure by measure.

We arrived after crashing through open ocean swells, one hour's journey across the bay from our base in Pemba. The villagers, young and old, swarmed to our boat. Once again they were thrilled to see Mama Heidi and our team, who always bring gifts of love from the heavenly Father. We carefully unloaded our cargo: a battery-powered sound system, gifts for the children and lots of lollipops and drinks.

Heidi busy giving gifts

Together, we climbed the hill to the simple school and church we had helped to build and had a joyful time, singing and praising the Lord of all Creation. Our very close friend, Mel Tari, from Indonesia, preached on his experience of being found by Jesus on a very remote island in the Pacific. Heidi helped us put on a skit, which was hilarious and moving for the children. We passed out candy and drinks and gave each child a backpack and flip-flops.

A great highlight was giving out awards for the best students of different ages at the little school in Londo. No one here had any education until the school was built. Everything had to be provided from scratch: books, papers, pencils—and a teacher! We have since added an adult literacy course and now the older gentlemen and ladies are reading for the first time.

Jesus has not forgotten Londo! He is sustaining us through many challenges so that we can continue to love the village and reach many more Mozambicans in this wild, remote province of Cabo Delgado. We feel as though we are just beginning to see what God can do.

It is time to go. We climb into our boat and wave good-bye to our amazing village family in Jesus. We will be back. They have even built Heidi and me our own mud hut, just so we can stay longer. We head toward the open ocean. Once again the big swells crash against our boat and soak us with spray. We see the powerful wind and water of the Holy Spirit in these waves and pray for all the more.

American Thanksgiving in the Bush

Our team is standing in a village courtyard way out in the bush. It is dark, but stars cover the sky and the moon is shining brightly. It is a beautiful night. Our faithful generator is running, powering the sound system and one strong floodlight. Heidi, standing on the big truck, is silhouetted against the light, very excited, telling stories animatedly to illustrate the Gospel. The whole village is listening; all the children are sitting up front paying close attention. They have been singing and dancing as only Africans can, and clouds of dust still hang in the air.

Most of these villagers are already enthusiastic believers, and a church has been established here. We love to revisit our churches and keep the Holy Spirit fires burning. As always we pray for the sick, and two are healed; one is the son-in-law of the village pastor. Both have been deaf for years and now they are learning to speak. The power of God is made known, and increased faith rises up from the village to heaven.

Heidi and I are invited to the pastor's hut to eat and are moved deeply by an unexpected Thanksgiving dinner. There is nothing in the hut but a plain table, little wooden chairs, a rope bed and a few changes of clothes hanging on a clothesline. We learn that our hosts have done the most special thing they could for us. Once a year they eat chicken, and tonight they have killed their one scrawny little chicken to honor us. We each get a tiny piece or two and enjoy delicious chicken sauce by dipping cakes of ground cornmeal in it.

We are soaked in the rich love of God as we partake of the very best this pastor and his family have to offer. Finally, we take our leave and with great thanksgiving we go to our tents and fall asleep for the night. All is quiet and Jesus is with us.

We wake early, sweating as the rising sun heats our tents. After coffee, bread and lots of fellowship, we gather with the villagers to dedicate their new children's house. Where possible, we are developing a system of church-based orphan care, asking each pastor to take care of a dozen orphans. We gather in the house to pray with our orphans, who are not orphans anymore, but *fully adopted* into the family of God and by the Body of Christ in this village. The pastor, his wife and the new children under their care are beaming. We pray that our emerging child-sponsorship program will help support these children and thousands more like them all over Mozambique.

Outside of the children's house there is another surprise. Muslim leaders in their caps and gowns have come to the village from the nearby mosque. They heard about the deaf being healed the night before, and they want prayer, too! They bring us extravagant offerings: a pair of doves and a rooster. They are touched and healed as we pray in the name of Jesus. They grin with pleasure, and we leave them with a solar-powered audio Bible. May greater knowledge of the cross and the love of God continue to spread across this province.

Heidi: Rain is pouring down through the thick trees all around us. A throng of Mozambicans huddles together, tightly packed as they try to stay out of the rain. Plastic and canvas sheets have been spread out from the church roof, held up by sticks and poles, to keep the rain off as many people as possible. But the downpour is heavy, conditions are wet and miserable and the whole situation is a very unlikely setting for revival.

We are having a bush conference in Inhambane Province, which we have rarely visited, and people have come from hundreds of miles around. They are hungry, physically and spiritually, and I am praying that the Holy Spirit will make the most of our time together—however the enemy tries to dampen the occasion.

The rain is loud and the people in the back standing in the mud can hardly hear us. What can the Holy Spirit do here? Plenty! Right now He is cleansing the entire assembly of demonic oppression. Tears are running down faces and bodies are shaking. Hands are lifted high. A huge cry is rising up to heaven. I have just asked how many are being harassed and afflicted by demons, and nearly everyone stands. Mozambique is riddled with witchcraft and demonic power, with so many going to witch doctors and then God in a confused attempt to meet their desperate needs.

Now I have asked the people to confess whatever is wrong in their hearts so that they can be cleansed and protected from the power of evil. The Holy Spirit comes in force, and I cannot be heard over the sound of repentant voices crying loudly for mercy and help. We lay hands on as many as we can reach. We rebuke all evil power. Finally, a mood of great peace and relief settles on everyone as we move gently into the remainder of our service.

At one point the electric power quits, leaving us sitting in the dark with only the sound of the heavy rain. So the people sing without a keyboard. Their pure, powerful voices blend uniquely African harmony and rhythm. This worship is spine tingling. Our little, muddy, wet conference has become a taste of heaven on earth.

After a few days we leave, flying in our little Cessna due north toward Sofala Province. We are full of wonder at our huge, far-flung Mozambican family, now more than ten thousand churches strong. The Holy Spirit miraculously binds our churches together, giving us a united heart for a transformed society of humble, Spirit-filled believers, saved only by the blood of Jesus.

Bicycles for Jesus

Our pastors have been waiting patiently for years and now a church in Curitiba, Brazil, has provided dozens of bicycles for them—and the bicycles have just arrived! Some of our pastors have been walking ten, twenty or thirty miles a day to plant churches, through the rain and mud, dust and heat, day and night. Now they can preach and plant churches all over Nampula Province.

It is dark, hot and humid. Our poor, but large city church is packed tight, lit by a few bare bulbs. One by one the pastors are called and make their way forward to receive a bicycle. We lay hands on and anoint each bicycle, praying that angels and the power of the Holy Spirit will accompany our pastors wherever they go.

Many have been raised from the dead in this province and the name of the Lord has become well known among the desperately poor who frequently face illness without medical care. Demons fight all they can, but they are being pushed back. Tonight I preach and call the hungry forward for prayer. We missionaries and pastors lay hands on as many people as possible. The Holy Spirit touches them as He wills, according to their faith and desire. One young girl is thrashing on the floor, possessed by an evil spirit. She is delivered as one of our Iris missionaries, Antoinette, prays over her and comforts her until she is calm and peaceful. As she smiles with quiet joy, the girl is given a beautiful vision of heaven!

Late in the night our team finds a little restaurant still open and once again we reflect on what God is doing among us.

Against all odds and in spite of every hardship, God is pouring out love, patience, endurance, determination, faith and vision into pastors in this province, enough to accomplish miracles of growth that we never expected years ago. Our appetites are growing. *The more He does, the more we desire!* May His presence in this province never stop growing.

Graduation!

Next we come to graduation day for our Harvest School of Missions and Harvest Bible Schools. It is marked by a tremendous day of worship at our Pemba base, blending black and white, rich and poor, foreigners and nationals as we mark the end of almost three months of classes and outreach.

Missions school graduation in our prayer house

We experience wild celebration, hearts bursting with praise! Many are experiencing the intense power of the Holy Spirit and a kaleidoscope of His emotions. Faces are dripping with perspiration, but are full of joy. Missionaries are praying for pastors; pastors praying for students; students praying for teachers; everyone praying for everyone!

Our speaker, Mel Tari, celebrates the significance of this day in God's plans for each pastor and student. It is exhilarating to watch our village pastors sing, "Go, go, go!" They will go—to the uttermost parts of this nation, carrying the Gospel with all the love and power they have been given. We pray for their safety, health, strength and anointing as they face every kind of challenge. We pray for our mission students as they follow their calls throughout the world. Many are interviewing for long-term service with Iris. We are so *deeply* blessed!

Following Our Leader

I have learned a secret! It has taken me thirty years, but now I believe I have it—and of all places, I learned it in a Jacuzzi! I have learned to be content. I am taking hold of that for which Christ took hold of me. I am learning to know Christ and the power of His resurrection, to have fellowship with Him in His suffering.

I am learning to see what He sees, to go where He goes, to feel what He feels—just to follow the Leader. I am becoming like Him in His death and somehow attaining His resurrection. I am pressing on and I will not stop. I will stay in this body and bear fruit. I will continue to take hold of that for which Christ took hold of me. He looks at you and me and He says, "I want you!" He died to take hold of *you*. He died on the cross so that you could live as He lives. What a Savior!

I will forget what lies behind—all the sin, all my mistakes, every time when I did something stupid—and I will press on, looking forward to the prize, heading toward victory. And while I am doing all this, I will rest because I have learned this secret.

I was working with some people who have very little. We were out in the dirt ministering to men, women and children who are in great need. My hosts wanted to bless me, so they booked a hotel room for me—a suite, actually—with a Jacuzzi. Now, I did not want a suite with a Jacuzzi because I thought the money should go to help someone else. I asked my hosts to move me to a Motel 6.

By making that request, however, I was actually offending their hospitality. Honestly, it can be quite hard when you are coming and going from the mission field—beans and rice then a sumptuous buffet, no food then food, no water then clean water. The Lord said, *Stop, Heidi. You need to stay here and get into the Jacuzzi and soak!*

"Soak, Lord?"

Yes, receive.

"Okay."

So I thanked my hosts for their generosity, sat in the Jacuzzi and watched the beautiful warm, clean bubbles. Water does not come from a tap where we are, and if it does come out it is green and you would not want to soak in it. Often we are out living in a tent in the "bush bush." There are no toilets, not even a hole in the ground, and everybody is watching you do everything.

But the Bible says, "I know what it is to be in need, and I know what it is to have plenty. I have learned the secret of being content in any and every situation." In all things, we can rejoice. In every situation, He will provide. He will not leave us burned out and discouraged, tired and overcome.

As we spread His Kingdom, we find that His grace is sufficient. We can do all things—working *and* resting—through Him, through His strength.

Time to Reflect

I know what it is to be in need, and I know what it is to have plenty. I have learned the secret of being content in any and every situation, whether well fed or hungry, whether living in plenty or in want. I can do everything through him who gives me strength.

Philippians 4:12–13

12

Christmas in Pemba

"The best yet!"

Rolland: This dark, rainy day is unusual for Pemba. Despite the clouds, summer is upon us in the Southern hemisphere, and our cooling fans feel good in the heat and humidity. No white Christmas here, but we have been celebrating the season in our own way and spirits are high. In a few days Heidi and I will leave for California to spend Christmas with our own children, but now it is a joy to reflect on how the Lord has blessed our Iris family here in Pemba as we celebrate Christmas early. The ocean before our house is a stormy gray, but the Holy Spirit has been with us in all His radiance and peace.

For Christmas we took our children to the beach and had a great party. It was a brilliant day, with warm breezes and rustling palm trees. Of course, there was lots of running, jumping, flipping and splashing as the children played in our awesome Pemba water. Then we all got together for hilarious games. It was fantastic to watch bright smiles and hear all the laughter.

Christmas fun and games on the beach

Heidi had organized some simple costumes and props so that some of the children could put on a nativity play, right on the beach. We held races in the sand, and the children ran with all their might to the finish line—a line of missionaries waiting with open arms to hug them. Finally, the suspense was over as we passed out hundreds of bags of wrapped presents along with drinks. May the Holy Spirit continue to look after each one of these children and raise them up in the knowledge and love of the Lord.

Later we gathered at Maringanha, our new property on a wild, undeveloped stretch of beach a few miles from Pemba. We have built a big, round, open, breezy prayer house with a thatched roof there, and when I arrived it was already packed with construction workers, guards, cooks, teachers, house-parents, administrators—everyone in our Iris family who works for us.

Many had never experienced Christmas or the generous, gracious heart of God until they came to Iris, so Heidi and I were determined to give them the greatest time possible. We set up a generator and sound system, and started dancing African-style with abandon. This last year we produced our own Makua worship CD, and we had it playing as loudly as possible!

We had a blast into the late afternoon. Then, as we were treated to a fantastic African sunset over the water, we blessed and thanked our workers for all their labor in the Lord. After a very special chicken and rice dinner we plugged in a floodlight and kept celebrating and worshiping the Lord. Finally, Heidi and I sat together on chairs, and we kissed and hugged each worker according to African custom as each came and received a gift. Today we have again tasted and seen that the Lord is good!

Sunday Christmas Celebration

We start church at eight in the morning with prayer and intercession. By nine or ten the crowd always swells with men, women and children from our center and all over Pemba. Church is never predictable. Different groups sing and dance. We worship with all our hearts. Foreigners and Mozambicans pray for each other. Our children lay hands on our visitors and bless them.

Today is very special. Our Mozambicans are putting on a Christmas play with angels, shepherds, Mary and Joseph, a horse, goats and hay, a manger and a real baby Jesus! Many of our Mozambican visitors know very little of the Bible, but this drama will settle the story of Christmas into their hearts. A wave of worship sweeps over the people as we revel in God's amazing, overwhelming gift of His Son to the world.

Three outreach teams from our mission school just arrived back in Pemba after ten days in the bush going from village to village. They are overcome with excitement. The blind saw, the deaf heard and food was multiplied three times. What a privilege it is for us to be able to bring the Good News to Pemba in such a vivid way!

This Christmas we appreciate more than ever the beautiful, international family that God has formed among us here. Let's long for *more* faith working through love—the only thing that counts. Together let's press on to what lies ahead: the best yet!

Being Like Him

Heidi: His divine power is everything we need. We can have faith in the power of the living God. We can take that faith into our homes, our workplaces and our mission fields. We can see through the devastation and the suffering to the opportunity for God to work in *every* situation we find ourselves in.

Suffering is seeing what Jesus sees; joy is doing what Jesus does. So when Jesus sees hunger, He offers a little boy's lunch to His Father and gives it to His disciples and *they* feed the multitude. Jesus wants to release *you* into your divine destiny. There is not one person exempt from this, including *you*, even if you have not given your life to Him yet. Meet Jesus and become who you were meant to be. The moment you give your life to Him, He will give you something to do and the means with which to do it well!

Sometimes in the Church we have pushed people down and out because of selfish ambition. The Bible says this: "Do nothing out of selfish ambition or vain conceit, but in humility consider others better than yourselves. Each of you should look not only to your own interests, but also to the interests of others" (Philippians 2:3–4).

Do nothing out of selfish ambition. We should not make our sons and daughters wait until we are dead before they are released. We *already died* and we *have been raised* from the dead, so let's run together, beloved.

His divine power has given us everything we need for a life of godliness. *He calls us as His own*, by His own glory and goodness. God is calling us, His sons and daughters, to participate in His divine nature—we get to be like Him! He is asking us to partake of Jesus, to eat enough to be strengthened and full, to eat and drink of Him every day so that we are not weak or in despair.

Baptism in the Indian Ocean

And once we have eaten and drunk, to give His Body to others, fresh Bread from heaven. We are called to multiply what we have received, to carry the glory and divine nature of Christ Jesus.

Let's ask Jesus to help us see; ask Him to open our eyes; ask Him to strengthen us and fill us. Let's ask Him to make us ready by His glory and because of His goodness, so that we can be *with* Him and *in* Him. Christ in you, the hope of glory. How wonderful to live like that!

Time to Reflect

His divine power has given us *everything we need* for life and godliness through our knowledge of him who called us by his own glory and goodness. Through these he has given us his very great and precious promises, so that through them you may participate in the divine nature and escape the corruption in the world caused by evil desires.

2 Peter 1:3–4 (emphasis added)

PART 3

GOING EVEN LOWER

13

Pressing On to the Best Yet

"He is able and willing."

Rolland: It is spring, and Heidi and I are back in Pemba. Since January we have been traveling on an intense ministry schedule all over Asia, to Europe and across Africa. It has been a thrill to see the power of God fall on hungry believers all over the world. The Body of Christ is getting more and more desperate for God, willing to pay any price to experience His Presence and companionship. There is no pleasure like walking and talking with Him, leaning on Him alone for every possible care and desire of our hearts.

How much more of Him do we want? He is able and willing to pour out His Spirit without measure. May we never lose our appetite for more righteousness, peace and joy in the Holy Spirit. All these are found only in our magnificent Savior, with all the intensity and fire of the author of life Himself.

This is not the time to be hindered by doubts, divisions and politics in the Church. We do not have room to worry about titles, positions, credits and recognition. We cannot be frustrated with concerns over support and publicity. We have no idea how to engineer revival. We are utterly dependent on our God. What we have already seen and heard has raised our expectations to new heights. He is able to keep us and *finish* what He began in us. We can trust Him with our hearts, our spirits, our health—anything that has to do with our well-being.

His power among us knows no limits. He baptizes us with His Spirit and all things are possible when that happens: deep conviction and repentance, sobs of love and gratitude, tongues and prophecy, waves of heat, purest peace and refreshment, super hunger for the Word of God, visions and visitation, revelation, healing, floods of heavenly joy, insatiable longing, wrenching intercession, singing in the Spirit, angels all around, weakness under the tangible, heavy weight of His glory, a sense of wonder and awe at His presence.

We love His gifts and all the touches and demonstrations of His love. They all propel us toward the ineffable goal sought by Christian mystics for centuries: *union with God!* "But he who unites himself with the Lord is one with him in spirit" (1 Corinthians 6:17).

When fruits of character are joined by gifts of power, truly our lives reflect His glory and presence. We need His love in our hearts. We also need His anointing to accomplish anything. We need both His Word and His Spirit.

We are still learning to go lower still, which is the only way forward. And we are still learning to stop for the one in the middle of a sea of need. We are still learning what it means to be a friend of God and value fellowship with Him and each other above all else. We are not professional, high-powered, efficient missionary machines. We measure the quality of our lives by the depth of our relationships. We are learning to love.

Recently, as I mentioned, we were in Asia. We cannot talk about all the things we saw and did and the places we went, but we can say that we sense a rising tide of desire for God that is opening the way to revival that will increasingly transform the nations of Asia. There are huge ministry opportunities there. The multitudes are ready. The time is ripe for harvest. Time after time we saw crowds of hungry and desperate people surge forward to be touched and healed by the power of the Holy Spirit. The churches were incredibly generous to us in helping with the needs of the poor.

Churches in Singapore and Korea, with whom we have developed close relationships over the years, especially encouraged us. They were so fervent, responsive and eager to help. We also had a terrific time in Taiwan, where I spent so many years growing up. This is Taiwan's hour. There is a stirring and rising up that is fresh and exciting. We took part in a major conference in the Taipei Arena that was a historic milestone for the Church. May such hunger and seeking after God be met with more and more outpourings of the Spirit.

From Asia we made it back to Pemba in time for that month's birthday party on the beach. The children were so excited to race and play, kick soccer balls and celebrate with cake and Coke—and lots of presents! They love to pray and worship, too, and we are hugely grateful to Jesus for transforming and enriching their lives thoroughly in every way.

We also had time to revisit Londo and the village we described earlier that can be reached only by boat. Transformation has come to their isolated habitat, with the school and church, solar Bibles, a teacher, schoolbooks and pens for the children and, most importantly, knowledge of the Lord! It was a joy to meet with them, and teach and pray with them far into the night. On the floor, in the light of one dim bulb powered by our generator, we felt the rich presence of the Lord invade all our joyous

Children in Londo village, holding new school supplies

Giving tablets and candy to children at Londo village

hearts. Later, drifting off to sleep in prayer on our rope bed in our very own mud-grass hut, Heidi and I considered how much wealth Jesus has brought to this simple, bare, primitive village.

It was great to wake up in the morning and emerge to beautiful skies, a gorgeous ocean and a village full of people who have become family. Simply relating to them in the Lord is the stuff of the Kingdom! They, of course, also need the power of God in every way and every day, so we continue to pray for their extreme needs. In Jesus we will keep ministering to them in word and action—this last people group to be reached in Mozambique.

The Work in Sudan

Recently, I made my first visit to our base in Yei, Sudan, led by our young, energetic, anointed and very happy Michele Perry, director of Iris South Sudan. Yei is not much more than a collection of dirt roads and shacks, and the south of Sudan is barely functional, severely diminished by many years of war. But to us it is an exciting frontier that is showing what only God can do.

In the bush near Yei, Michele and her missionary friends and national helpers have built an attractive children's village and primary school. So far this is our leading Iris ministry in southern Sudan. Through faith in God, they have persevered though hardships, threats and dangers of all kinds, and now have a center full of the love and presence of God.

Arriving in Sudan from Uganda, on a dirt airstrip

Here, as in Mozambique, needy children have been gathered into the Father's heart and now are filled and thrilled with the life of God. Their brilliant smiles, laughter, worship and play are a portent of the life of heaven from a child's point of view. We keep learning how to be as humble and believing as a child!

We also held a conference for Iris pastors and leaders from around southern Sudan, plus any who wanted to join us in seeking the Lord together. Eyes were opened in a fresh way to the fire and presence of the Holy Spirit, and hearts widened to receive all the teaching we could bring in a few days. Earnestness, brokenness and crying out to God on the floor were combined with an upbeat taste of the joy of the Lord. Intensity, freedom and abandonment began to replace programmed order in a way the attendees had not seen before. Knowledge of the head became knowledge of the heart. To top it off, God multiplied food when a hundred unexpected children showed up at a lunch. Everyone had plenty and a lot was left over!

Religious legalism, restrictive tradition and doctrinal confusion have crept into traditional churches over the years, even in the bush, and nominal Christianity is often the norm. Righteousness and the purifying fire of God must overcome corruption and profiteering in the Church all over Africa. *By example*, leaders need to resist strongly and categorically the witchcraft that is so prevalent—and even mixed deceitfully into the Church. In this conference we took up the challenge to pursue holiness, without which no one will see the Lord.

We are proud of our Iris family in Sudan and will count it a privilege to encourage them all the more as we pursue revival all over Africa.

Our leading pastors in southern Sudan

One Church at a Time

Heidi was ministering with great grace, favor and the presence of the Lord in Switzerland and France while I was in Sudan. We returned to Pemba and were glad to be ministering again to our own family here in our "hometown." It is a rich experience to watch local Mozambican mamas with their babies and brightly colored clothes pray their hearts out at the altar along with our missionaries, staff and many children. Jesus knows just exactly how to touch each one with what he or she needs at the right moment. We will not be satisfied until *everyone* we encounter is saved, filled and healed!

Just yesterday we dedicated yet another new village church near us along the ocean. It was a rough ride over a very rutted dirt road in our Land Rover, but we arrived in the village to find an excited band of believers waiting eagerly for us. They were so proud of their new mud-and-thatch building. From the youngest to the oldest they all celebrated and praised God with bright, laughing faces. We prayed the Lord's richest blessing on them, dedicating the building, the pastor, the people and the whole village to the service of God.

This is a significant breakthrough, because not so long ago this village was very much opposed to the Gospel; Heidi was stoned there. After a deaf man was healed, they dropped their rocks and slowly opened their hearts to the Lord Jesus. And so the family of God is growing in this whole province, one simple church at a time.

After the dedication, we all began filing down a footpath to the beach for some baptisms in the ocean. It was a brilliant African day with dazzling cloud formations spanning deep blue sky over an even deeper blue and very warm ocean. As faithful worshipers sang and danced on the sand, one by one our new believers waded out to Heidi and our Mozambican pastors and were baptized. With upraised arms and shouts of joy they came out of the water, consciences washed clean in the blood of the Lamb. *New creatures*, created in Christ Jesus for good works! Overcomers, heirs of the promises, destined for glory and eternal life. Heidi said the water was hotter than a bath and many little sea creatures stung her, but it was worth it!

Our inspired and contented party returned through bushes and trees back to the village and everyone feasted on beans and rice for lunch. Spiritually and physically fed, the village is ready to press on in Jesus. Remoteness and poverty will not marginalize this resting place of the Holy Spirit. May "the least of these" receive the *best*.

More Like Him

Heidi: I have little to give, but I will give the little I have to Him. God loves it when we put the little that we have into His offering. He does not mind that it is only a little; He loves that we give what we have. And even though we have only a little to give Him, we can give Him everything. Not just a tenth of our lives, not half of our lives, not even 99.9 percent, but *all of us*. We can be like tiny seeds hidden away in the dirt, hidden deep in the heart of God waiting for His life, His beauty to shine on us and through us so we can bear fruit. Like seeds that fall down to the ground—fall from His love and His mercy, lower still. Seeds sown with tenderness, grace and compassion. Little lives laid down into fruitfulness.

My heart cries out, "Oh, Lord, let me be undone!" I choose not to stand up, grow up or get a grip. I want to fall down. I want my hands and my heart to stay loose, yielded into His heart and His love. It is about being made *more like Him*, not more like me.

I will contend to be undone. I will ask Him to help me stay undone. Not finished, always ready, always wanting to be more like Him. His life and His love poured into my empty life, to fill up and overflow from this little jar of clay.

What is a Christian? Someone who is *like Christ*. Maybe we are not Christians yet, but by God's grace we are becoming

Christians, becoming more like Him. Growing smaller rather than growing up. Going lower still until we become nothing and He becomes everything.

As we move in this direction, we will understand more and more why His love requires that *the first shall be last and the last shall be first*. As we look with His heart and His eyes to the lost, the broken, the empty, the orphans, those who have had everything taken from them, as we start to put them first, doing nothing to promote ourselves, but doing everything out of His love and for His glory—then we are becoming more like Him, Jesus, who gave up everything to become like us.

Jesus: the King of glory who made Himself *like us*, who humbled Himself and became nothing, taking on our form—human likeness. Jesus: the One who was born like us, who gave every day of His life, His every and last breath for us, who poured out His life, even His blood, so that we might have life and life eternal. He became like us so that we might become *like Him*: transformed, utterly and completely altered, no longer the same. The very life of Jesus poured into our empty vessels, our little jars of clay. This, my friends, is all we must aspire to be.

Time to Reflect

But we have this treasure in jars of clay to show that this all-surpassing power is from God and not from us.

2 Corinthians 4:7

14

Enjoying Our God

"More love and joy."

Rolland: Is revival normal? The Westminster Shorter Catechism was written in the 1640s by English and Scottish divines to educate laypersons in matters of belief. It is part of one of the grandest doctrinal statements to come out of the English Reformation. It is composed of 107 questions and answers. The most famous question and answer in the Catechism is the first:

> Q. What is the chief end of man?
> A. Man's chief end is to glorify God and to enjoy Him forever.

After thirty years of missionary work, Heidi and I understand more than ever that God wants to be our greatest pleasure. He is most pleased with us when we are most pleased with Him. And when He is pleased with us, He grants us the desires of our hearts (see Psalm 37:4).

Our whole aim as Christians, and as Iris missionaries, is to glorify God by everything we think, feel, say and do. For us this finds expression particularly through ministry to the poor and to "the least of these." By giving the cup of cold water, feeding the hungry, clothing the naked, inviting the stranger in, healing the sick and visiting those in prison, we love and serve Jesus Himself (see Matthew 25:31–46).

But there is more. We do this through the grace of God *and* the power of the Holy Spirit. And here begins the controversy. There is an attitude that sees fiery revival and a life of miracles as the rare exception, not to be expected in normal Christian living. The idea is that most of what God does in the world is done in a natural way through the holy virtues of dedication, hard work, faithful endurance, sacrifice, generosity and compassion. That we should learn to live most of the time without the miraculous, overpowering intervention of God, and prove our love for God by our quality of character.

We understand that our foundation is the righteousness of God, freely given to us in Christ. But then we learn that to love God and appreciate Him is to long for His presence. Here we make a decision. As in any love affair, we love everything about God, and we choose to treasure any way in which He manifests Himself. We desire more of God continually and will never settle for distance from Him. The great outpourings of the Holy Spirit in history are beacons to us, always giving us hope for an even more abundant life in Him. They are not meant to be hopelessly out of reach for the rest of us, but to spur us on to all that is possible in God.

So we enjoy the full spectrum of God's dealings with us and are always pressing forward to what lies ahead—to even more of God. Jesus died so that our relationship with God could become natural. So that *all He is capable of* supernaturally would become natural and normal for His people.

All the good work we have been able to do in this movement in Africa has been sparked, fueled and sustained by the fire of revival and the supernatural. We never could have gotten to this point—ten thousand churches in total and ten thousand children cared for—without miracles all the way. "Life is more than food, and the body more than clothes" (Luke 12:23). The Holy Spirit gives us rivers of Living Water that flow out of our innermost being. We love and enjoy all the manifestations of God's Presence and find that as we take more and more pleasure in God, we are filled with all the more strength and motivation to do His will through good works.

Short-term visitors praying for the many sick in the village

We do what we do because of visitations, visions and the pouring out of His Spirit upon us. We are excited and keep going because the dead are being raised and the blind and deaf are being healed. The poor come to Jesus, whole villages at a time, because they see the power of God's love. We are financed because God grants supernatural generosity to thousands of people without appeals from us. We are awed and thrilled that God would tangibly enter our meetings, touch our bodies and fill us to overflowing with love and joy—inexpressible and full of glory. We are on fire because He does more than we ask or think.

It is very simple. We desperately need revival, all the time. As I have said before, Heidi and I would both be dead now without miraculous healing. Every day we face need, pain and suffering that cry out for more than any human can respond to. Our own hearts pant for the living God as the deer pants for streams of water (see Psalm 42:1). We are *made for God*. We are made for revival. We are made for the glory of His Presence. We must encounter Him.

So we say, more revival! More fire! More signs and wonders! More gifts of the Spirit! More intimacy! More love and joy! More fruit! Let's find every lost sheep! Let's take in every orphan! Let's share the Kingdom! And let's never settle for average, mundane or normal!

In short, let's totally enjoy our God.

The Fruit of Revival

Heidi: The work before us is huge. We can do nothing without Jesus and without the Body of Christ, so we invite everyone to labor with us in every way possible. Revival has fruit. It brings transformation, and God uses people to bring it.

We are not just soul winners and definitely not just social workers. We are after the Kingdom. For us, revival includes relief and development—with a difference. We trust God and aim for His glory in everything. He is utterly practical. In nearby Mieze we are establishing a model community as an example for the rest of our movement. We are emphasizing micro-investment and entrepreneurship.

We are drilling all the water wells we can in bush villages. We have housing projects. We want to expand agriculture. We have a vision for a university offering the poor an education that provides job skills in tourism, business and information technology. We are opening a child sponsorship program to greatly increase the number of children in our care. We are planning a relief arm of Iris that can respond to disasters around the world. Every kind of initiative and help is needed.

Heidi and villagers pumping at a new Iris well—a tremendous event

Once again we are so grateful for our amazing Iris family who, without pressure, continue to support and help us in our work with faithful, sensitive generosity from God. We are all blessed!

Becoming Likeminded

Scripture says:

> Therefore if you have any encouragement from being united with Christ, if any comfort from his love, if any common sharing in the Spirit, if any tenderness and compassion, then make my joy complete by being like-minded, having the same love, being one in spirit and of one mind.
>
> Philippians 2:1–2

Are we united with Christ? Does our relationship—the love that we have for Jesus and the love that He has for us—does this love encourage us? Do we find comfort in His love? Does the Holy Spirit minister to us with tenderness and compassion? Does this love make us more like Jesus? Do we have the same love for others as He has shown to us? Do we have any tenderness when we are shopping at Walmart, any compassion when we go out for a bite at our favorite restaurants? Does the fragrance of Christ flow from us when we stop to get gas or when we check out of a hotel?

I was hungry this morning and wanted some breakfast. Quite often with our schedule there is no breakfast, no lunch, no dinner. Just this one day I wanted breakfast, and it did not happen. I was a hungry jar of clay! I wanted to be full and I was empty. Being emptied out can cost you breakfast. It can cost you time that you do not have. It can leave you so weak that you cannot stand up. But when we are weak, guess what: He is strong! His power is perfected, fulfilled, made complete in our weakness.

> But he said to me, "My grace is sufficient for you, for my power is made perfect in weakness." Therefore I will boast all the more gladly about my weaknesses, so that Christ's power may rest on me. That is why, for Christ's sake, I delight in weaknesses, in insults, in hardships, in persecutions, in difficulties. For when I am weak, then I am strong.
>
> 2 Corinthians 12:9–10

My prayer is that you and I would become more united and more like-minded with Christ, having the same love that He has. That we would encourage like Jesus, comfort like Jesus, have the same tenderness and compassion as Jesus. So that whomever we are with and wherever we go—if we are shopping or with our kids or worshiping or working—we will be like Jesus.

Sometimes we can look at each other and think, *I wish I were more like that person. . . . I wish people would notice me like that*. But God values our lives as they are, hidden in Him, and He knows what is best for us. In reality, you may not want to be like the person you think is doing better than you.

You are at your best when you are hidden deeply inside the heart of Jesus. Never do something because you are looking for the approval of man. Your heavenly Father is the only One whose pleasure is worth having.

Time to Reflect

Do *nothing* out of selfish ambition or vain conceit. Rather, in humility value others above yourselves, not looking to your own interests but each of you to the interests of the others.

Philippians 2:3–4 (emphasis added)

15

Revival as Missions, Pure and Simple

"We conquer by taking the low road."

Rolland: Jesus is our focus. We stay on track through all the differing ideas and streams in the Church by maintaining this simplicity and purity. Paul wrote: "I am afraid that just as Eve was deceived by the serpent's cunning, your minds may somehow be led astray from your sincere and pure devotion to Christ" (2 Corinthians 11:3).

We fix our eyes on Jesus, the author and perfecter of our faith. When pressed to the absolute limit, as was Paul, we determine to know *nothing but Jesus* and Him crucified. He is the only basis for our confidence. He is the dividing line, the stumbling block, the cutting edge, the point at which we meet salvation and life.

No one in the universe is more controversial.

We trust and love Him because He died for us and rose again on our behalf. He is the One who suffered for us. He paid the penalty for our sins. He purchased our lives with His blood. He showed us what love is. And so we are loyal to Him alone. We *belong to Him* and not ourselves. We make it our ambition to please Him. If necessary, like Paul, we will suffer the loss of all things in order to have Him. We forsake every temptation in this life that takes us away from Him, even slightly. He is our greatest pleasure, our ultimate companion. We no longer love the world or anything in it, because He is the supreme object of our desire. Worthy is the Lamb!

We rejoice that we participate in His sufferings, so that we may be overjoyed when His glory is revealed. To the end of this age we will endure evil opposition and glorify God by overcoming with faith, which has been proven to be genuine. In all our troubles, our joy knows no bounds. As aliens and strangers in this world, we look forward to our perfect inheritance, kept in heaven for us.

In heaven Jesus will be exalted for His obedient suffering and, in the same way, we will share in His reward. We conquer by taking the low road. We gain life by losing it, for His sake. We humble ourselves under the mighty hand of God that He may exalt us at the proper time. We learn to love by laying down our lives for others and, in so doing, minister to God Himself.

It is impossible to be devoted to Jesus and not share Him, pure and simple. We cannot see Him now, but God has ordained that *we love Him by loving each other*, whom we can see. He is love and we cannot separate the first commandment from the second. There are many callings, but none higher than to give water to the thirsty and food to the hungry. The intercessors at home and the troops in the trenches are equals in the Kingdom. We learn to love just as we are gifted and called by God.

Mission is our joy. Mission is also the simple, logical outcome of knowing Jesus. We have life and hope; others do not. We have reason to rejoice; others do not. We have love in our hearts; others do not. We have food and clothes; others do not. We have health; others do not. We have family; others do not.

We have no reason to be anxious; others are weighed down with cares. The calling of every believer in Jesus is to have a share in correcting these imbalances.

That may take us across the street or around the world. We should be utterly available to God to go anywhere and do anything at any time. He can and will make a way as He leads us. That is the testimony of Iris Ministries, for every one of our thirty years.

We begin each day by immediately exercising our faith in Jesus to attack every problem and pressure we have. We cast all our anxiety on Him because He cares for us. This sets us free to rejoice in Him always and take a positive view of everything. Then we pray for the greatest, most miraculous, victorious day ever! And on we go through the rest of the day, loving and worshiping Him as we use our gifts, natural and supernatural, to bless everyone we can, as deeply as we can.

To us *mission* is the natural outworking of our faith. It is the way we return the love God has for us. There is no other option. Revival without mission is deficient. To turn away from the lost, poor and needy is to turn away from God. Our intimacy with Jesus extends to one another. Such is the excellence and perfection of His Kingdom!

A Landmark Bush Conference

Dust hangs thick in the air, a shining cloud illumined by the bright daylight pouring in from outside. I can hardly believe we are breathing it. Rhythmic, pounding feet are kicking up every loose particle on the cement floor. Fire is in the atmosphere. Perspiration is pouring down every face. Life is in the building! Our Mozambican bush believers are dancing their hearts out, celebrating with all their might at the dedication of our new church building in Mieze.

It was nine years ago that we came to the province of Cabo Delgado and started the Pemba base. The predominant Makua people group here was considered virtually unreached and unreachable. But the Holy Spirit backed us up with power and kindled great hunger for God among the poorest of the poor—as we have seen Him do over and over all these years. Our second church plant was this one right here, just twenty minutes by road south of Pemba.

Since then our pioneering Mieze body of believers has developed into a forerunner for the rest of our churches across the province, which now number more than 1,700. We can hardly keep up! The Mieze church has become more than a simple mud hut with meetings on Sunday—it has become a modest prototype of community development and transformation that continues to progress every week. Here we learn what is possible in God for the poor of this nation, how the Kingdom can have impact on every aspect of life in a village.

The Holy Spirit came to Mieze years ago, and His fire is blazing brighter than ever! The holy Presence of God is manifested here in a beautiful kaleidoscope of ways, including the healings that the people have come to expect and receive regularly. His Presence looks like deepest conviction, tears of desperation, repentance, longing and relief; quiet, glorious, weighty worship; and also the most energetic joy of the Lord, dancing before the Lord with all our strength!

Behind the scenes in the kitchen at our large Mieze conference

His Presence in the bush of Africa also looks like homes, schools, farms, food, water wells, family, adoption of many children, fellowship, miracles, fun—the full spectrum of life in God. Today we can also celebrate this brand-new building, in Mieze, the precious fruit of a lot of hard work and patience flowing from the vision of our Pastor Juma and our director, Dr. Kantel. It is utterly simple and basic, but large and exciting—a community center of faith and hope in a sea of poverty.

We have very special visiting speakers, a working sound system (sometimes!), a worship team from Pemba and the Presence of Jesus Himself. Outside we have pitched our new evangelistic tent, covering more gatherings for children and special groups. Crowds have converged on us from all directions out of the bush, filling the church already, and with solemnity and exuberance we are dedicating this physical building for the use of the Master, just as He chooses.

Out of the darkness of isolation, paganism and witchcraft has risen a great light—a people given over to Jesus—and today we are thrilled. May Mieze show the way for the rural poor throughout our Iris family. Transformation is coming, in Jesus' name.

The Gospel in a Wild Bandit Town

Heidi: It is cold inside my tent. I have a cot, which keeps me off the lumpy floor, but a crossbar is jabbing me in the back, and it is hard to relax. I am zipped up in a sleeping bag with a tiny pillow trying to get comfortable somehow. I pray for a long time, just going over with Jesus what has happened tonight.

The dirt courtyard outside is covered with tents, all colors and shapes. We have a contingent from our Bible school and missions school camping for an overnight outreach here in Namanhumbir, which has been called the most dangerous place in the province, maybe the country. All is just simple mud huts in this small town, but its reputation is known far and wide.

Our unsaved Mozambican friends in Pemba are horrified that we are here. This place has a long history of out-of-control violence, as the haunt of ruby smugglers who come from as far away as Somalia and Thailand to seek their fortune in gemstones, however they can. Only recently has the government begun efforts to tame its wildness, illegal trade and banditry. Children are sold for less than ten dollars. Sex slaves are pregnant at eleven years of age. Murders are frequent. Rich ruby deposits in the area have produced a den of evil in the otherwise beautiful and peaceful bush of central Cabo Delgado.

We already have a church and pastor in Namanhumbir, but our leading Iris pastors in nearby towns have long prayed for a spiritual breakthrough here, and that we would bring teams to challenge the dark forces of the region. Tonight we had our second outreach in the town, after bringing in a big truckload of students on a long trip from Pemba. We showed the "Jesus Film," as always, which had the complete attention of more than a thousand viewers, including many children in the typical rags of Mozambican poverty. We preached our hearts out and the response to the Gospel was enthusiastic, yet again.

We always pray for the sick at these outreaches, and usually significant miracles rivet everyone's attention. We did see physical healings, but tonight was unusual because the greatest need among the crowd was for deliverance from evil spirits and alcoholism. It is common here for demons to choke people by the throat in the night. Our team laid hands on everyone within reach. Relief and joy spread through the throng as the power of the Holy Spirit set one oppressed soul after another free. *Jesus is the answer, always, for everything!*

Our little camp, so conspicuous among mud huts, has settled down. Most of our budding missionaries and local pastors are asleep now. I ask Jesus to post angels all around us for protection. Many hearts have opened to Him tonight, the bound and oppressed taste the thrill of freedom in the Spirit. Our pastors are happy and we have taken a significant step toward the transformation of this community. We are amazed at how fast revival is spreading in northern Mozambique. We live to bear fruit and we thank Jesus for such a privilege.

At first light in the crisp morning we wake to the quiet chatter of curious village children, standing all around as their visitors emerge from the strange-looking tents. Breakfast is coffee, bread and jam, such a luxury here. Nobody is in a hurry as we relax and discuss our outreach and the unique challenges of this place.

But more happened last night than we realized. I am seated over in a corner under a grass roof interviewing a young man who has a testimony. He is the nephew of the village chief—and he will never be the same. Since he was a small boy of around eight he has never heard a sound. He was at our meeting watching everything, but hearing nothing. I prayed for him and then, as he slept, he had a vision in which a man in white came to him and put drops in his ear. This morning he woke up hearing perfectly and able to talk again! I explained that the man was Jesus, and now we have another fervent believer among us.

Heidi hearing the testimony of a boy totally deaf for many years, completely healed after Jesus appeared to him in the night

We have to leave by bush plane to other meetings, but we do not leave the team alone here and arrange for them to be taken to a safer town for the night. We encourage our pastor in the area and decide to meet with his people away from threats at his church building. We all hike down a long dirt path past many ruby smugglers to a large, beautiful pond outside of town. We worship the Lord freely in the wild open beauty and baptize new believers among the flowers and lily pads in the cool water. Even those hardened men we met along the way softened as we stopped for them, too. We cannot have enough of revival here!

Back in Pemba, our Mozambican friends outside our church are beginning to understand why we deliberately go to dark, dangerous places where there is so much suffering. We are not afraid. God's love is not powerless, and we bring His Presence with us. Every day we apply our faith and look forward to even greater demonstrations of what He alone can do. So pray with us as we appoint a strong team to return to Namanhumbir and bring more of His Kingdom!

Our faith has grown stronger over the years and so Jesus is allowing us to face even greater challenges. We pray you will share our excitement at what the Holy Spirit will do next among us, continuing to overturn the worst Satan can do in the earth. Our labor and steadfastness are not in vain. Let's run the race to win and press forward together to the best yet.

God's Big Love

The Bible says that love *always* hopes. God always delights in us. He sees the very best in us and loves us to go for gold. So forgetting what lies behind, we press on to the mark of His high calling. What is the mark of His high calling? Love, love and more love.

His love is big enough to touch any life. His love is able to transform *evil* back to front until it spells *live*. You do not have to die in darkness or depression, anger or pain—rather let Him hold you and speak hope and courage to you, until you are ready and able to *live* in His love.

There was a boy in the north of Mozambique that we heard about because he raped a little girl. He was a mentally disabled boy who did a terrible thing. When I heard about him, I just felt the Holy Spirit reaching out to him. I had to find that boy. Nobody wanted me to find him. They said, "Heidi, we are warning you—this one you cannot have."

But God's love is big enough to touch any life, to make light out of any darkness. Jesus came that we might have *life*, so that no more would we have to die in depression, anger or pain. He loved people back to life. He would go anywhere, talk to anyone. And wherever He went, He would stop for the one—the forgotten one, the one who was rejected, outcast, sick, even stone dead. Even a thief who was dying for his crimes on the cross next to Him. In the Kingdom of God's love there is *no* sinner who cannot come home.

I prayed about this boy: "Please, Lord, let me have this one." I flew all the way from the south of Mozambique to the north looking for him. And eventually I found him, and then we took him in. That boy who did a terrible thing is a picture of God's grace. Oh, that we might be so given over to His loving grace that *nothing* would come between us and the one in front of us!

I believe that Jesus would have given His life for just one person. Jesus emptied Himself, He humbled Himself and He so yielded Himself to His Father's love that He had no ambition of His own. He was not looking to build an empire, He did not want praise or adulation or to impress people with who or how many followed Him. He stopped over and over again for just *one* person, for just *one* life.

God is looking for laid-down lovers who will give themselves up for just one person. I truly believe that in heaven, your reward will be just as great if you really loved one person, as if you saw a million people give their hearts to Jesus.

Will you lay down your life for love? Will you intentionally give your life over to His love?

Time to Reflect

Love is patient, love is kind. It does not envy, it does not boast, it is not proud. It is not rude, it is not self-seeking, it is not easily angered, it keeps no record of wrongs. Love does not delight in evil but rejoices with the truth. It always protects, always trusts, always hopes, always perseveres.

1 Corinthians 13:4–7

16

Our Core Values

"Love is not powerless."

Rolland: Pemba is an unlikely spot for a leadership conference aiming for global revival! Hidden away in our cozy little African prayer hut on the beach, however, with stiff ocean breezes whipping our crude canvas walls, we gathered together to represent our worldwide Iris family. We met with God and melted together in His Presence, far out of town on a rough, sandy road under a clear, brilliant African sky by day and a bright moon by night. The natural environment felt wild, raw and peaceful; the spiritual environment marked a milestone in our Iris history.

For the first time our key Iris leaders came together from bases all around the world, to pray, soak, worship, dream and find unity together. More than one hundred missionaries and nationals from dozens of countries descended on little Pemba in our remote corner of Africa. For days we ate and drank, wept, laughed and celebrated together as we built each other up in faith with our encouragement and testimonies. Our guest speaker, Bill Johnson, brought depth and God's holy presence with him.

We were awed as we began to grasp the extent of what God has been doing among us and the strength of our family bonding. We, a missions-oriented body, are enjoying God and our life of service to Him to a degree Heidi and I never anticipated thirty years ago when we first headed for the mission field.

The meetings were a great opportunity for us as leaders to articulate as never before what it is that makes Iris "Iris." The word is Greek and also Portuguese for "rainbow." Heidi and I began ministering as a Christian dance-drama ministry called "Rainbow Productions." We saw our different creative talents as colors of a rainbow that the Son shines through, giving a beautiful result.

We "contend for the faith that was once for all entrusted to the saints" (Jude 3) and have never tried to emphasize anything that is new, unique, clever or different. We try not to be controversial. We share with all Christian streams what no born-again believer can argue with:

- the glory of the simple Gospel
- repentance and faith in Jesus
- the simplicity and purity of devotion to Christ
- avoiding anything that would empty the cross of its power
- when backed against a wall knowing nothing but Christ and Him crucified
- seeking righteousness that comes from faith
- being transformed through adoption by our heavenly Father

- understanding faith working through love as the only thing that counts
- living with the hope of attaining to the resurrection from the dead

As we changed course from being an itinerant evangelistic ministry to intentionally stopping for the poor, we became more and more holistic in our approach to missions. We had no choice. When people are thirsty and starving, the holiest thing we can do is offer a cold drink of water and fresh bread. But we are not just social workers; we have *fresh Bread* that comes down from heaven, Jesus Himself. Our ministry is never finished. "We proclaim him admonishing and teaching everyone with all wisdom, so that we may present everyone perfect [fully mature] in Christ" (Colossians 1:28).

In the process we find that we cannot just be an orphanage or a church or a Bible school or a humanitarian aid organization. We cannot just hold bush conferences, plant farms and engineer micro-investment. We cannot just specialize in education and technical assistance. As a broadly based international family, we must embrace all of the above and more, sharing Paul's attitude in Acts:

> However, I consider my life worth nothing to me, if only I may finish the race and complete the task the Lord Jesus has given me—the task of testifying to the gospel of God's grace.
>
> Acts 20:24

Necessary Controversy

Even so, we have discovered that some key elements of our lives and ministry in Jesus, although absolutely necessary, are controversial. We think they should be normal in the Christian life and in Christian ministries everywhere—not special and unusual. Heidi and I started out naively in these areas, but have come to realize we must prize, protect and nurture these values in our hearts and impart them to others. If we lose *any one* of these values, Iris would not function and be what it is today. When all these elements work together, it is as though there is a spiritual chain reaction, generating life and heat in the Spirit!

The following five values are not the only critical ones to us, but the Holy Spirit brought them to the forefront of our minds at our leadership meetings.

1. We understand that we can find God and can experience intimacy, communication and companionship with Him in His Presence if we share His love for righteousness.

Missions is generally portrayed as an unromantic endeavor: Pursue disciplined obedience to the Great Commission. We have been taught that prayer is hard work, feelings are irrelevant and getting the job done is what counts—that we do not need spiritual experience to proclaim the Gospel; that we cannot expect immediacy and intimacy to be normal; that we can function without His manifest Presence.

We feel the opposite. We have gone through enough fire and hardship to know that "you will seek me and find me when you seek me with all your heart" (Jeremiah 29:13). Without actually *finding* God, in fulfillment of Jeremiah 29:13, we cannot do what we do. We cannot love with supernatural, unstoppable love unless we actually experience the love of the Father for us first.

As the radiance and exact image of the invisible God, Jesus is a spiritual lover, our perfect and ultimate companion. Our first value is to know Him in a passionate relationship—with love that is as strong as death (see Song of Songs 8:6). We major

147

first of all not on mission strategy, methods, projects and fund-raising, but on *having the God-life* that the world so needs and craves.

But neither are we attracted to mindless, impersonal mysticism, experience without content and relationship. We pursue passion and truth, not serenity with no actual basis for happiness. We relate to God with both our minds and hearts. We engage with Him and find life and joy in our interaction. When we find Him, we find and gain everything. Without Him, we can do nothing of real value.

2. We are totally dependent on Him for everything, and we need and expect miracles of all kinds to sustain us and confirm the Gospel in our ministry.

When facing great human need with our human frailties, we rapidly reach the limits of our resources, wisdom and love. We face overwhelming poverty, sickness, demonic attacks and every kind of evil. But with excitement and joy we look beyond what we can imagine doing in our own strength. We run into the darkness looking for Good News because it is the power of God that gives the world hope. We do not apologize for seeking and valuing God's power, because without it love is incomplete and ineffectual. Love is not powerless.

Heidi and I began our life of missions with the dream of living out the Sermon on the Mount, taking Jesus at His word that *we do not have to worry about tomorrow*. We imagined addressing extreme human need by example, living without anxiety, free to bless always with pure motives, looking to God alone for what our hearts and bodies need. We would turn neither to the left nor to the right to gain support. At every obstacle our only confidence would be in the cross of Christ and the conviction that God is thrilled to be trusted for miracles along our way.

Heidi praying for the deaf

Believers from the bush in prayer at a conference

We still believe that we experience miracles because *we value them and ask for them*, understanding that He will give them to us only if they will not take us further from Him. For His sake we lose our lives daily, knowing that by His power we cannot lose, but will be sustained and become more than conquerors.

The engine behind the growth of Iris Ministries in Mozambique has been a marriage of love and power. We do not have to choose between them, but we can look forward to doing even greater works than Jesus, while remaining in His love.

3. **We look for revival among the broken, humble and lowly and start at the bottom with ministry to the poor. God chooses the weak and despised things of the world to shame the proud, demonstrating His own strength and wisdom. Our direction is always lower still.**

We are not experts. We have not learned how to "do" church and revival. We know only to humble ourselves under the mighty hand of God (see 1 Peter 5:6). We gravitate to the low things of the world. Competition and comparison with others will never suit our DNA. We feel no pressure to succeed and excel, but we exult in doing things well by the power of the Spirit.

149

God's ways are the reverse of the world's ways. We spend our time on those who have no influence. We focus our attention on the few, stopping for the one. We show that God cares when no one else does. We go to the neglected, the forgotten and the lonely. We will go anywhere, if possible, to minister to the meek and desperate, the poor in spirit, to those who truly understand their need of God.

> 4. **We understand the value of suffering in the Christian life. Learning to love requires willingness to suffer for the sake of righteousness. Discipline and testing make saints out of us and produce in us the holiness without which we will not see God's face and share His glory. With Paul we rejoice in our weaknesses, for when we are weak we are strong. Under great pressure we learn to rely on God, who raises the dead (see 2 Corinthians 1:9).**

Jesus was rewarded for enduring evil opposition without sin. Our reward in heaven will be for the same—doing the will of God. We resist sin, to the point of shedding blood if necessary, by considering His example (see Hebrews 12:3). Jesus is glorified now not because He exerted His power over His enemies, but because He overcame them with love. That kind of love entails suffering—the willingness to turn the other cheek, go the second mile, deny ourselves, pick up our crosses and follow Him. He showed us the only way to be counted worthy, and the angels sing of him: "Worthy is the Lamb, who was slain, to receive power and wealth and wisdom and strength and honor and glory and praise!' (Revelation 5:12).

There is no shortcut to our heavenly inheritance: "Now if we are children, then we are heirs—heirs of God and co-heirs with Christ, if indeed we share in his sufferings in order that we may also share in his glory" (Romans 8:17).

> 5. **The joy of the Lord is not optional, and it far outweighs our suffering! In Jesus it becomes our motivation, reward**

and spiritual weapon. In His Presence is fullness of joy, and with Paul we testify that in all our troubles our joy knows no bounds (see 2 Corinthians 7:4). It is our strength and energy, without which we die.

The supernatural joy of the Lord may be the most controversial of our core values! But our aim is to impart so much of the Holy Spirit that people cannot stop bubbling over with love and joy. We pass through conviction and brokenness, even daily, but we are not left there. The Kingdom is righteousness, peace and *joy* in the Holy Spirit (see Romans 14:17), in that order. And in His joy we are all the more capable of compassion for others, unfettered by our own sorrows.

Heidi and I could never have endured this long without a river of life and joy flowing out of our innermost beings. We are not cynical and downcast about the world and the Church. Instead we are thrilled with our perfect Savior, who is able to finish the work He began in us. We gain nothing by being negative, but we overcome the world with faith that we can cast our cares on Him.

Joy, laughter and a light heart are not disrespectful of God and incongruous with this world, but are evidence of the life of heaven. We are not referring to cheap and foolish levity that ends in grief, but exultation in the truth and reality of our salvation, a powerful work of the Spirit.

In these days we identify more and more with the captives of Israel who were brought back to Zion:

Our mouths were filled with laughter, our tongues with songs of joy. Then it was said among the nations, "The LORD has done great things for them." The LORD has done great things for us, and we are filled with joy. Restore our fortunes, O LORD, like streams in the Negev. Those who sow with tears will reap with songs of joy. He who goes out weeping, carrying seed to sow, will return with songs of joy, carrying sheaves with him.

Psalm 126:2–6

Riots in the Streets

Earlier this month riots broke out on the streets of Mozambique's capital of Maputo, as many people were protesting their increasing hardship due to soaring prices. The cost of bus tickets doubled in price, bread prices rose by 30 percent, and a 110-pound bag of rice climbed to half a month's salary for the average Mozambican with a job—in a country where there is only 14 percent employment! On top of that, the country's currency has greatly devalued. It is very difficult for a nation that has to import so much to survive.

People disrupted life in the city by blocking traffic with bricks, stones, pipes and trees; upturning and burning buses; burning cars, tires and gas stations; throwing rocks at cars and smashing windshields; and attacking any who tried to break the blockade carrying passengers.

Police using real bullets to control
the rioting in Maputo

Police moved in against stubborn crowds with tear gas and began to shoot with both rubber bullets and live ammunition. Ten people were killed and three hundred injured. Schools (including our own), businesses and the airport were closed down. The violence threatened to spread to other cities around the country.

Things have calmed down now, but these recent events keep us aware that Mozambique, now the world's sixth poorest country, is still a land of desperate poverty for most people. We have seen a huge number of people come to the Lord and great blessing come to many, but we must press on until the Gospel covers the land. Join us in faith and pray for peace, safety, godliness and prosperity in the face of tremendous challenges and demonic opposition.

For fifteen years we have seen increasing revival in Mozambique. We will not stop now! Jesus, finish what You have begun and make Mozambique a model for Africa in fulfillment of Your promises. In the Kingdom of God, the best is always in the future!

Losing One Airplane, Gaining a Better One

For ten years I have written stories about how revival has spread all over Mozambique. In part it was because our donated Cessna 206 light aircraft allowed us to hold frequent bush conferences and do relief work at great distances from our home base.

Mozambique is a huge nation. Its coastline would stretch from Mexico to the panhandle of Alaska. Roads are few and most are very rough and nearly impassable much of the year, even with four-wheel-drive vehicles. Without the plane, time and wear-and-tear on vehicles would have kept us from the majority of our ministry. We used the Cessna heavily and I enjoyed flying it as my personal prayer cathedral in the glorious skies of East Africa!

But the devil tries to resist all that we do, and one night Cessna N4744F, my gift and hug from God, met its end. At the time I was not in Mozambique. Our plane was being flown from Pemba by an American commercial pilot, Andrew Herbert, to a service in South Africa.

Near the end of one leg of the trip, while Andrew was beginning a descent from eight thousand feet in the dark into the city of Beira, the propeller broke free from the engine, and the plane lurched virtually out of control.

Diving at two thousand feet per minute and struggling to keep the plane level, Andrew faced a forced landing in the pitch-black night. Even with the plane's landing light on, Andrew could see nothing and plowed into trees in the bush. The plane was completely destroyed, but miraculously Andrew survived with nothing more than a bad cut on his chin!

The pilot miraculously survived and walked away after hitting trees in the dark

Wreckage of our Cessna 206 in the bush

The crash happened at around seven p.m. For hours and hours, friends from Beira searched for the wreckage, driving through rivers and swamps, getting stuck over and over, asking villagers along the way if they had heard or seen anything. Finally, they were directed to the site and found Andrew at two a.m., alive and so grateful to God for sparing his life.

Aviation authorities are investigating the prop failure, which occurred after the plane was cleared to fly following routine maintenance. This is a reminder that we are in a serious and ongoing spiritual battle. We need and value your prayer and intercession in every way.

Our hearts and attention are now turned to the promise of a brand-new airplane, a Quest Kodiak, which we will take delivery of early next year. This is a high-performance ten-place turboprop specially designed for missionary bush situations. Its speed, payload, ruggedness, utility and short-field performance are just what we need!

We are engaged in a great struggle for souls in Africa, knowing that our warfare here, as everywhere, is not against flesh and blood, but against spiritual forces of wickedness in heavenly places (see Ephesians 6:12). Our battle has been indescribably intense in recent months, but at the same time we rest in our perfect Savior, who sustains us through the prayers of so many.

Our greatest gratification comes from seeing the Holy Spirit fill so many spiritually hungry hearts with love and joy all over Mozambique, in addition to our new and growing Iris bases around the world. We understand that with such great fruit also comes the reality of disappointments, attacks, personnel challenges and tragic failures. These will not keep us from being overjoyed with all that God has done among us. We live to experience His Presence and to see Him bring about what only He can accomplish.

Your Place in the Battle

Heidi: There is something about becoming nothing that makes for real happiness and peace. Rolland has found this out so beautifully. He has come to know the joy of not having to *be someone.* We do not have all the answers, but God does. We are not the answer, but God is.

All God wants us to do is lay our lives down into His. Do you know how much stress disappears when you finally decide to stop trying to figure everything out and let Him lead you, day by day?

> Jesus gave them this answer: "I tell you the truth, the Son can do nothing by himself; he can do only what he sees his Father doing, because whatever the Father does the Son also does."
>
> John 5:19

This is Jesus, the Son of the Most High God, telling us how to become nothing. Jesus did only what He saw the Father doing. He did only what God told Him to do. What a burden that removes from us! We do not have to figure everything out, be everywhere and do everything. All we have to do is what God is leading us to do.

What is God leading you to do? Encourage your spouse or friend, plan something special for someone in need, go to Columbia, adopt a child, care for someone who is unable to care for himself? We have only to give the little we have. He is not expecting more. God takes the little we have and multiplies it.

Why not start every day by asking Him to show you what He wants you to do today? Just one day at a time. If we decide in our hearts to let God lead us and to have no ambitions of our own, *He makes the way.* We do not have to make everything happen any longer. Why not rely on His strength rather than our own? His power is made perfect in our weakness.

When you are a child, you do not expect to plan your own life, find your own nourishment, be wholly responsible for everything. We are His children and here He is, holding His arms wide, asking us to trust Him to lead us and provide for us. I do not lie awake at night worrying how I will feed all the children we care for. Why? Because they belong to our heavenly Father. That means I am free to do anything, go anywhere, as long as I know that He is leading me. Before anything else, beloved, we are His children.

Do you know that because you are His child, you are free? Free to love as many or as few as He calls you to love, free to clean toilets or climb on a plane, free to do anything He wants you to do. We are free to serve the One who is worthy, in any way He chooses, even unto death (see Philippians 2:8).

We can give our lives away with great joy and peace, knowing that we are losing nothing. And it takes such a load off your shoulders if you no longer have to worry about who you should be, where you should be and how you are going to get there.

Time to Reflect

"My command is this: Love each other as I have loved you. Greater love has no one than this, that he lay down his life for his friends."

John 15:12–13

Heidi helping a totally healed girl learn to speak after being deaf and mute since birth

PART 4

NOT BY MIGHT

17

On the Road with Iris

"Jesus is alive! He is here!"

Rolland: Yesterday Heidi and I arrived back home in Pemba, really dirty. Hot, perspiring, clothes soggy; feet caked with dust and mud. We really looked like missionaries! Our creaking old Land Rover was loaded down with Mozambican ministry friends and a couple of short-term visitors.

We were returning home as one big, happy family after pouring out all we could on another visit to a village in the bush. With piles of equipment and supplies stuffed between us, on our laps and under our legs, we had been talking nonstop about the sheer joy of serving the people here. We are rich indeed!

The Land Rover is slow and top-heavy, but utterly practical for us. The big, heavy, flat-roof rack easily handles all our tents, sleeping bags and other overnight gear. Its long-travel coil-spring suspension takes us almost anywhere, despite the deep ruts and mud. This is our missionary machine and our teams drive lots more like it. Outreaches like this are the mainstay of our ministry, part of our weekly routine. But what God does on these outreaches is anything but routine.

In the face of all of Mozambique's problems, deep revival has been taking root all over the northern province where we now live. The devil may point to all kinds of faults, but we just boast in our weaknesses (see 2 Corinthians 12:9) and revel in the sheer power that God has displayed among us in recent years. We are pleased with His workmanship and extremely encouraged. It is obvious that this transcendent power belongs to God and does not come from us (see 2 Corinthians 4:7).

This Is Missions!

Our outreach began two days ago. First we sent out two four-ton flatbed canopied trucks carrying our main group of visitors and Mozambican ministers. These trucks haul our sound system, projection screen, generator and whatever else we need. All our equipment is banged up, dented and covered with dirt, but it keeps working. Our team is treated to the sublime experience of bouncing for hours over rough roads, cooking in the heat, sitting on the hard floor of these trucks—a privilege not to be forgotten!

The lead group arrives late in the afternoon and gets busy putting up a little tent village, so curious to rural Mozambicans not used to such conveniences. All they need is a grass mat to sit on! Then our intrepid revivalists hook up a generator, sound system and video projector, now with the whole village flocking around, anticipating another Iris night under the stars with God the center of attention.

It is hard now to find a village where we have not ministered. We have been coming to this particular village for three years, and every time we keep adding to the villagers' understanding and experience of the Gospel. We are excited and awed by what has happened among this one tribe, now with around two thousand churches.

Our follow-up group arrives after dark. The "Jesus Film" is being shown, and we can spot the glowing screen from far off. We have the film memorized in fine detail, but the whole village is there to see it once more, mesmerized and motionless. Many cannot read, but they will never forget the film. It is just amazing how that soundtrack has been produced in so many languages, even in our local Makua, here at the ends of the earth.

It is dark, but for the light of the projector. No moonlight, but millions of stars. These villages have no electricity, flashlights or batteries. Visitors can be spotted with their glowing LCD headlights nodding around and startling flashes going off from their ubiquitous pocket cameras. By now our African friends in this village know about our teams, and they are good sports. The end of the movie shows the disciples bowed in worship of Jesus and we turn on our floodlights. This really strains our generator!

Heidi jumps to life, her appealing, rich voice ringing out in Makua and Portuguese, to the great delight of the people. *Jesus is alive! He is here, and we can have the best night ever with our Perfect Savior.* Our team energetically acts out the story of the Good Samaritan, which makes a permanent impression in this culture. It seems as though everybody wants Jesus among these people, once considered so dark and unreachable. Most want the Holy Spirit. Most want better hearts, more love and joy, more of His Presence. We are not ashamed of enthusiasm. To us, meetings are a time for emotional release, a gift from heaven, African-style. And the Holy Spirit backs us up.

Many want healing prayer, so our team spreads out and lays hands on the sick. As we have been to this village so many times, the needs are relatively minor. But one man is completely healed. He had been hard of hearing in one ear and totally deaf in the other. In recent years we have seen a stream of people healed of deafness nearly every week!

The villagers are always amazed and encouraged that people will travel so far and spend so much money to come and bless them. They know we come with no ulterior motive and they feel *honestly loved*. After the meeting, they return our love by giving us their best in the form of food.

That night we brought with us our usual spaghetti and tuna fish, but they surpass that easily with their gourmet bush chicken. Really, we have never tasted better. They explain how they do it. First, you have to kill the chicken—very important—then you pluck it and gut it, yes, yes. Toss it in the pot over the fire and stir: cha-cha-cha-cha. . . . Then when it goes *schhhhhhhh*, you know it is done.

And the amazing part: They come up with tomatoes, onions, garlic, spices, on and on, until they produce an *unreal* sauce that we cannot get enough of. How do they get all these ingredients in the bush so far away from any cities? They put out a big plate loaded with white mealie cakes, and we launch into the chicken pot and keep dipping away at the rich, reddish-brown juices. But eating like this is really very rare, saved for absolutely the most special occasions.

Finally, at midnight we get into our tents, zip them up tightly and try to kill every last bug we can with the spray we always bring. I thought I would read the Bible and write, but I was way too tired. This is enough Kingdom work for one day.

The day starts early in the bush. At the first glimmer of dawn, village kids crowd around our tents excitedly to see who may emerge. Sure enough, out come bedraggled foreigners with mussed-up hair and makeup, trying to find toothbrushes and the outhouse, which one of our number fell into! Soon we get collected enough to start serving hot drinks with bread and jam to our little foreign and national family. Under our overhanging thatch roof, with our view of the lush, wild African bush, we feel satisfied and at home.

Breakfast with our missions team at the village outreach

No village outreach is complete without meeting with the chief, agreeing to build another school and planning where to drill a well. Then we have morning church. Our Iris church buildings are usually mud-and-stick huts with dirt floors and a tin roof. This one was badly damaged by a windstorm and half the roof has been ripped off. No matter. A group of us gathers in our lowly bush tabernacle to enjoy the Presence of God together. Spine-tingling African drumming is *de rigueur* for our meetings, with energy and dancing to match. Soon a flood of children pours in. We never swat them away as so many do in Africa. We put them in front and minister to them. We grown-ups have to learn to be like them or we will not even get into the Kingdom. Our unlikely revival spot in the bush pulses with the life of heaven.

We preach, making the Gospel as clear as possible, emphasizing always the righteousness, peace and joy in the Holy Spirit that come by faith in the power of the cross. We pray and the

Holy Spirit falls on many visitors, missionaries, pastors and even the village chief himself. God graciously fills us with more love and joy than we can express. May God have no competition in the bush of Africa. May He be the greatest pleasure in the lives of these precious saints who trust so simply in their perfect Savior. We revel in His power to deliver us safely into His heavenly Kingdom and to be with us all the way.

Teaching children in a remote village

A critical ingredient of any bush outreach is our discipleship time with a select group of local believers. This time Heidi sits under a tree with the village's leading Christians, by now her close friends, and teaches quietly and unhurriedly from the Scriptures. This is a really valuable time, in many ways the highlight of the outreach. Earnestly and hungrily everyone asks questions, seeking more understanding. Many have already been to our Bible school in Pemba, and they keep pressing on to the best yet. Our aim is far more than feeding or numbers, but to "present everyone perfect in Christ" (Colossians 1:28).

While Heidi is teaching, our team members spread out all over the village to visit people in their huts and to pray for the sick. The villagers are so touched by these visits, and, in turn, the visitors are deeply moved by the reality of extreme poverty combined with the faith and joy of people who have almost nothing but Jesus and each other. Their spirits well up with a generosity that could come only from heaven.

Our outreach finishes with a gourmet lunch, again proudly produced and offered to honor us to the maximum. How can we respond to such golden hearts? *Yes, we are seeing revival*—with simplicity and purity that is breathtaking. How did we deserve the privilege of being here and witnessing God at work like this? Godliness with contentment is great gain, and our people are at peace, yet we have so much more to look forward to in the future. Those who have, Jesus said, will be given *even more*. Mozambique is headed onward and upward.

The men stay in the back but listen intently

On the way home, we stop at the local state prison and get another taste of what only God can do if our focus is on His Son. Revival has been breaking out under the ministry of Ania Noster, a longtime Iris missionary and close friend, and Ezekiel, an ex-prisoner. The prison interior is grim, dark and claustrophobic, as expected. A few prisoners are still locked in their dirty, miserable cells, but most are gathered in a long, narrow hallway with high security windows.

On entry, we are greeted with shouts of praise, and with one voice the prison reverberates with fervent worship. We join in, amazed, as these "dangerous offenders" sing their hearts out to Jesus, their real reason for living, the hope of their lives, the joy of their salvation. Rarely have we ever seen such powerful evidence of a change of spirit. This is the road to transformation, the cutting edge of revival: Jesus, the One who died and rose again on our behalf! He is the perfect personification of the love and power we all need and only our faith in Him will overcome this world.

The atmosphere in that dark, horribly depressing place is extraordinary. In the same way, His presence in our most difficult times is all and everything we need. Our hope in Him is secure, our future safely protected and reserved for us. We may be in prisons of many kinds, but we have a Deliverer.

After the prison we drive the last twenty minutes back to Pemba, stopping just for fruit and snacks at a roadside stand. I am really itchy and uncomfortable with so much stacked up on my lap. I can hardly move. What a full day! I cannot wait for a shower and a cold Coke. And a good sleep. Another day in the life of Iris on the road. And another day of eternal life. In Jesus, the best is always in the future. . . . Stay tuned!

Where God Dwells

Heidi: God gave me an unusual sign not long ago. Rolland wrote earlier about the time I was in the hospital for a month with an out-of-control staph infection. I was hooked up to an IV drip for eighteen days. While there, I was given all sorts of advice. I had prophets telling me to stand up, so I would try to stand up.

Then people said God was telling me to lie down, so I lay down. Rolland was taught how to make some kind of ionic magnetic thing. I got herbal remedies and the cousins of herbal remedies. I appreciated everything everyone recommended, but in the end I concluded, *Lord, I think these remedies might kill me!* I got tired of making plans to get better.

I think this sickness was more than earthly sickness. I think it was a sign of what God is saying to us. We have flourished in the renewal movement, in the presence of God and the beautiful work of His Holy Spirit. We have worked like the Jewish people who were called to rebuild the Temple in Jerusalem. We have labored for years, through much opposition, on the road day by day.

Listening to the Gospel with fresh joy and total interest

But sometimes we need to be reminded that *we* are not building His temple: He is! Our bodies are temples of the Holy Spirit. Thus, *we are to be His resting place*, a place that is utterly given over to Him. We are called to fulfill His plans and His purposes, not to be half-filled but *fully possessed* by Him.

Satan is trying to destroy your destiny, God's temple. If he cannot use sin, he will use sickness or exhaustion. So we have to fight. But the way we fight is going to sound *extremely odd* to anyone who likes to come up with a plan. The way we fight is not to have it all figured out, planned ahead and sorted. In this case, planning is not the remedy for sickness or exhaustion. Obedience is. God is calling us to lie down spiritually—to let Him love us until we are full of Him, full of His love and His life.

For twelve years the Jewish people had been rebuilding the Temple, and they were exhausted. But God gave Zechariah this promise: *God Himself* would dwell with Zechariah and the people, right there in that place that had no walls, no earthly means of protection. For God sent this message to His people:

"Run, speak to this young man, saying: 'Jerusalem shall be inhabited as towns without walls, because of the multitude of men and livestock in it. For I,' says the LORD, 'will be a wall of fire all around her, and I will be the glory in her midst.'"

Zechariah 2:4–5, NKJV

God would fill His Temple and, thus, be the glory in Israel's midst. Put another way, His Temple would be the resting place for His glory. In addition, He would be a wall of fire around it to protect it. And so we must fight, not to *make* a temple but to *become* His temple. To become a resting place for His beautiful, holy Presence. To be fully possessed by the glory of the Lord. He is calling us not to run harder, but to lie down.

What is your destiny? Is it to attend a university, work in a hospital, live on a garbage dump, go to the nations? Wherever you end up and whatever you do, your destiny is this: *to be fully possessed by God's presence.* To carry His glory. Then, if you are in a university, in a hospital or on a garbage dump, you are His resting place, and all that can be there is life and beauty.

Time to Reflect

Do you not know that your body is the temple of the Holy Spirit who is in you, whom you have from God, and you are not your own?

1 Corinthians 6:19, NKJV

18

Children's Day

"See what God has done!"

Rolland: Our children could hardly sleep last night. Today we will celebrate a fabulous national holiday in Mozambique, *Children's Day*! At each base, our magnificent staff has been working for months to prepare a giant *festa*, a feast of feasts. There will be presents, food, dancing, games, singing, worship, love and prayer—all to rejoice at the life Jesus has brought to us.

Heidi and I get up early. Today we have to look and be our best! Cameras will be everywhere and our kids are expecting a lot of attention. We charge down to the center in our old, rattling, beat-up Land Rovers, still running strong. The whole property at Pemba is pulsing with energy. It is a perfect day. The sky is clear and blue, the nearby ocean peaceful, the temperature just right. Everybody has a job to do. Our kitchen workers have been up all night preparing chicken for lunch. Others have been painting and decorating rooms, wrapping presents, dressing the children, making certain everything is in order.

Now comes the time to shower love on each individual treasure that Jesus has brought to us. We start with our baby house. Every child gets a gift bag, huge hugs and playtime. Each present is pulled out with wide eyes and big grins. Many of these babies came to us ragged, skinny, starving and dying of malnutrition, but now we bounce their chubby bodies in cute outfits on our knees and marvel at their transformation.

We keep moving through our dorm rooms, going to the older children, starting with the boys. Each room is neat and comfortable, decorated with flowers, balloons and streamers, the walls painted with fun murals and Scripture verses. What a contrast to the broken-down huts and slums these children came from! We are so proud of our staff who spent so much time shopping carefully for each age group. Mama Heidi spends a long time with every single boy, making sure each one feels much loved. All our missionaries, visiting teams, mission school students and Mozambican staff—everyone is absolutely pouring him or herself out on the children on this, their most special day.

Now, time for lunch. Today we have a mega-production. We have invited thousands of village children from our surrounding community—the poorest of the poor we could find—who have never had such a feast. About four thousand children have arrived, and lines have formed clear across our big property. Feeding them will take all day. This is exciting! A feast here can mean only one thing: pieces of juicy barbecued chicken with Cokes and all the rice and coleslaw anyone can eat, a super-rare treat for most Mozambicans.

Our dining room is quite a scene: Foreigners and Africans of every age are all over the benches and floor. What a chaotic, wonderful mess! Bottles, scraps and plates are everywhere as we try to keep cleaning up. The kitchen assembly line is pumping out piles of yummy food hour after hour. In a poor, hungry nation, this is heaven on earth.

An assembly line for 4,500 people at one lunch

Chicken and rice and soft drinks—nothing better

In the middle of this culinary extravaganza, a group of our younger girls adds rich African-cultural flavor with a dance production they have been practicing for weeks. The drumming, the rhythm, the flashing, sparkling energy all contribute to an atmosphere of excited celebration. These children are alive, healthy, full of life and hope.

After lunch, Heidi and I visit our older boys and then our girls, one room at a time. They have been waiting patiently most of the day and now we give them individual attention. We are joyfully struck by the difference in outlook that these youths have since they first arrived at Iris. A few years ago, when asked about their dreams and aspirations, all they could imagine was simply enough food to eat, some clothes and maybe a decent place to live. Now, with bright eyes, they are brimming with positive ambition! What do they want to become? A doctor, an engineer, a pilot, a pastor, a teacher, an evangelist, a missionary . . . the answers flow. Mozambique is being transformed, one young life at a time.

This one day might seem like a brief, relatively insignificant and almost frivolous moment of time in our long history of struggling for the Gospel in this poor land, but it is, in fact, a vivid portrait of what God has done among us. The love of God has reached down into the lives of the least of these in this land, offering hope and a future, both in this life and the life to come. We are seeing His love manifested in countless real and practical ways. Right before our eyes we are witnessing the fruit of our years in Mozambique and we know that *this fruit will last.*

We are encouraged. God has brought us this far and He will continue to reveal Himself and His ways, here and in all the farthest corners of the earth, to the hungry and humble. Truly He has given us a down payment and a guarantee of what is to come in the next life. So by His grace the Gospel marches on.

Here in Mozambique, at the heart of Iris Ministries, we have already seen more of the power of God than we could ever have dreamed. We have received more than we could have asked or imagined. Yet Jesus keeps flooding us with more; there is no limit. God pours out His Spirit without measure. And so we press on to what lies ahead.

Here is a baby boy, blind from birth with eyes white and clouded over. He is healed in a flash before many hundreds of Mozambicans, students and visitors. This takes place in a cement-floored, tin-roofed Iris church in Mieze, near Pemba. And here we now have a thriving community of believers who have witnessed a stream of healing miracles these past few years.

This baby was blind with white eyes just minutes before

Our bases in Pemba keep growing, hosting a community church for thousands, a Bible school, a missions school, a children's center, a primary school and housing for hundreds of missionaries, students, staff and visitors. We are inundated with foreigners from dozens of countries, which is just what the Holy Spirit ordered, and hearts from around the world are being shaped for ministry to the poor. We are in a Kingdom vortex of supernatural activity, a sovereign work of God that sweeps us along in refreshing wonder and awe.

Of course, we are also tested and refined to the uttermost. Wherever God is active there are responses and reactions of all kinds. Some fail and fall by the wayside. Spiritually, we are deep in enemy territory and keep getting threatened with our ministry's annihilation. We sustain injuries and casualties, but our demise is greatly exaggerated. We move from glory to glory as we learn through our hardships to trust God, who raises the dead (see 2 Corinthians 1:8–11).

The dead *are* being raised, the lost *are* being saved, the hungry *are* being fed, the lonely *are* placed in families, the poor and hopeless *do* have visions; and dreams and love, peace and joy reign increasingly. All this is His workmanship and He is able to finish what He began. He is perfect and He will perfect us.

Our Bible school for bush pastors remains a joy to us. Students come to us for three months out of every year for three or four years, and by then they are truly immersed both in the Word and the Spirit. Then we have our fifth-year students, whom we call our "MMs" (Mozambican Missionaries). These are humble, mature, solid, fervent carriers of the Gospel, God's answer for this country, and their testimonies are a thrill to hear. Joy, visitations, healings, salvations, transformations of all kinds flow from them. We are so proud of them. They should be teaching our foreigners, including us!

Here is one of our heroes, Pastor Adriano, who has been used along with many others to raise the dead: "Our Harvest School of Missions, in Pemba, runs twice a year for ten weeks at a time and always produces an intensely close, joyful, filled-up, free and released family of potential missionaries eager to lay their lives down for love. We pray for power to accommodate and respond to all the interest and hunger coming from around the world. The place to learn missions is on the mission field, where every day we can put into practice what Jesus puts into our hearts. May He continue to call many from this rich pool of lives to help us finish the task of testifying to the Gospel of God's grace in the neediest places around the world."

We also have much to report from other Iris bases. We are seeing the birth and growth of a missions movement marked by a full-bodied appreciation of all that the Holy Spirit can do, sustained by the interaction of Word and Spirit. Our ambition is not for Iris, but for bearing eternal fruit that will bring pleasure to our God and Savior.

Elaina was a traumatized girl of fifteen when the UN brought her to our Iris base in Yei, Sudan. She had escaped to the Sudanese border after she had been abducted and brutalized by the LRA in the jungles of DR Congo. Elaina was tortured, she saw people killed in front of her and she was left for days at a time, tied to trees. When Elaina arrived she could barely sit up; she had no use of either hand. What she had was scars all over her body and a faraway look of fear and pain in her eyes.

After she had spent time with Michele Perry and the rest of our Iris family in Yei, we caught up with her again, relaxed and happy now, laughing with her new friends around her. Two months later she was back with her family in Aba, DR Congo, healed and restored in Jesus with nearly full strength back in her hands. One by one we keep seeing victims of Satan's cruelty brought back to life, *healed inside and out*, a picture of the joy of Jesus. If there is hope in Jesus for Elaina, there is hope for anyone, anywhere.

Jesus has been busy in Yei, as He has been everywhere in our Iris world. Here is a sample of the good news that our Iris Revival School students reported during our last visit to Yei:

Visitation: Two of our students went to visit one of our Yei neighbors, a Catholic man. Everyone in his family was seriously sick. God gave the man a dream the night before that two men would come to pray, and he saw Jesus coming with them. Next day our students turned up. The man was beside himself that strangers would come and pray. Everyone was healed.

Prison: The officials have been asking for prayer here. Our team prayed over each room because of evil tormenting spirits, and the demons left. Many prisoners came forward to be released from the pains in their bodies. When they chose forgiveness, these pains left. The team prayed for one man who was in pain all over his body. He had been in prison for six years, falsely accused, he said. The moment he chose to forgive his accuser, and with prayer, the pain left.

Hospital: God is healing so many people. The hospital, which had been full for the last three to four weeks, is now almost empty. There are very few sick people left to pray for. The nurses have been thanking our teams and asking not only for prayer, but for teaching to learn how to pray for their patients!

Hospital: One woman was lying lifeless on the floor in one of the wards. She had wanted to die and took poison that left her blind, deaf, mute and unable to talk or walk. John Sebit stopped with the team and prayed for her. Then they moved on to pray for a few more cases. On their way out of the ward, they ran into this same woman, seeing, walking, hearing. She introduced herself as Rose!

Hospital: One young boy had recently returned with his family from Khartoum in fear of the referendum taking place there. He fell out of a tree he was climbing and was left paralyzed and in pain, his legs twisted beneath him. Our students prayed for him. His pain left, his legs straightened. They stood him up and he walked.

Police Training: About a month ago we noticed the arrival of about five hundred police officers, training near our compound. They came from all over our state. One of our team members was heavily burdened for them and began to pray. One day when we were driving by, we had an overwhelming sense that we should stop. We stopped and one of our key leaders, John, jumped out and went and met the lead commander. The commander asked John, "Where have you been? We need your help. We need someone to tell us what to do with all the demonic attacks we are experiencing." The commander invited us to come and share with the students at his Police Academy. So we took our revival school team and preached there. Of the five hundred students, 495 decided to follow Jesus and we will be baptizing them all in our local, all-purpose community pond.

Dust and trash all over the streets in Yei

Baptizing in a community pond in Yei

Good News from Somalia and Northern Kenya

CNN states that 750,000 Somalians are in imminent danger of dying of starvation, and this may be just the beginning. Although the horn of Africa is experiencing its worst drought in sixty years, the worst culprit is politics. Again, our fundamental problem in this world is not poverty and disease, but sin. And Jesus is the *only* answer for this problem. We need to show what He is like through our faith and through practical help.

Sudanese slum dwellers desperately in need of God's love

Our Iris vision is focused on North Africa and the wildfire spread of revival from southern Africa all the way up through the north and on to Jerusalem. The obstacles seem unimaginable, but it is a thrill to do the impossible in His name. We have been getting used to it all these years.

Iris sent a scouting team into northern Kenya last month led by Naomi Fennell. Our longtime Iris staffer Ania Noster, along with Ben Church, is just back from four days in Mogadishu, the capital of a closed nation in the horn of Africa. Ania reports: "I am planning to go in again with one other person by the end of the year. I want to take in relief for the famine, although logistically it's difficult, as the militias kill for the food and steal it. So I am praying and getting in touch with some of my contacts in Somalia country to see how Iris Relief can best get provision in, even if it's through another agency right now. We want to provide food, measles vaccines and plastic sheets for makeshift homes as the rainy season is starting. As Somalia the country is an active war zone in most places, and white people and visitors get taken hostage often, we are not planning on taking in any bigger teams right now. While I was there, there was a group from France still looking for their friend who got taken hostage a couple of years ago. A journalist was shot dead in Mogadishu the capital just a few days ago and another injured. It's a nation ripe for the glory of God to invade. I can't wait to go back!"

New Frontiers for Iris

One of our Iris core values has always been to concentrate on *the least of these*—the poorest of the poor, the most desperate and unlikely in the entire world to experience anything good. Here our perfect Savior loves to display His matchless grace and power. Mozambique was our beginning in Africa, and Heidi and I will continue to make this the object of our greatest attention. But as Iris grows and Jesus adds workers for the harvest, we pray for fruit throughout North Africa.

Our cutting-edge frontiers are now South Sudan and the DR Congo, spreading to northern Kenya, Somalia and Ethiopia. May Jesus flood us with carriers of His glory to meet the challenge of destroying the works of the enemy among these millions. Actually, the country in Africa that now has by far the greatest number of undernourished people is DR Congo, in spite of its lushness and riches. Again the chief, underlying issue is rampant sin.

We dare to be exhilarated in spite of all the horror before us and the world news because we remain convinced that we have a perfect Savior in whom we can put all our faith. We are of no use if we feel crushed and discouraged. Our theology must remain intact and true. *Our power is in the cross of Jesus* and nowhere else. So we invade the darkness with the Word of the Lord and the blood of the Lamb.

Then he showed me Joshua the high priest standing before the Angel of the LORD, and Satan standing at his right hand to oppose him. And the LORD said to Satan, "The LORD rebuke you, Satan! The LORD who has chosen Jerusalem rebuke you! Is this not a brand plucked from the fire?"

Zechariah 3:1–2, NKJV

Heidi: We *cannot* fight our battles in the flesh, beloved. We have to run into God's holy, all-consuming fire because that is where we are safe. God's holy fire purifies us. It cleans all the dirt and drives out all the darkness. When we are in the center of that fire, God Himself is a wall of fire around us and we are safe!

Actually, it is an unfair fight. We have witch doctors standing outside our base in Pemba, sticking big pins in dolls that look like us, but we have no fear because it is an unfair fight. All the witch doctors, demons—all of hell does not stand a chance. We are burning brands plucked from the fire—His holy, all-consuming fire.

All we are called to do is *be* in God's presence, to *be* where He wants us to be. Like Joshua, we stand in His presence and the Lord rebukes Satan. We have nothing to fear when the Lord rebukes our enemy.

Joshua was standing before the Lord and he was not clean:

Now Joshua was clothed with filthy garments, and was standing before the Angel. Then He answered and spoke to those who stood before Him, saying, "Take away the filthy garments from him." And to him He said, "See, I have removed your iniquity from you, and I will clothe you with rich robes." And I said, "Let them put a clean turban on his head." So they put a clean turban on his head, and they put the clothes on him. And the Angel of the LORD stood by.

Zechariah 3:3–5, NKJV

All of Joshua's impurities—just like our impurities, our sin, all the evil and ugliness—are removed by the blood of Jesus, our perfect Savior. Will we walk in the rich robes that He lovingly gives, robes of righteousness and victory? We have no reason to cower. His love is fearless. Will we take the turban that He offers to transform our minds and our thoughts, so that we take on His thoughts, the mind of Christ?

All we have is given. It is all grace, we cannot earn His love. Will you become His resting place? Will you lie down, even appearing not to do anything that looks to be useful, if He asks you to? Just because you love Him?

He can do more in one day than we could in a thousand years, beloved. Yes to Jesus, no to striving. And He shall build the temple of the Lord!

Time to Reflect

"Not by might nor by power, but by My Spirit," says the LORD of hosts.

Zechariah 4:6, NKJV

Appendix

We are awed by the support we continue to receive. We truly do pray at all of our bases, *Give us this day our daily bread.* Sometimes it is last minute, but every day the Lord provides for us. Faith, intercession and generosity have overflowed in our lives and work. Countless hundreds, even thousands of lives have been profoundly transformed through those sharing in the ministry of Iris around the world.

With all our special relief and development projects going on, we need to express our great debt of love to those who support our massive regular commitments to feed, house and minister to thousands already being cared for in our African family. We have huge monthly budgets at all our main bases, and it is absolutely and amazingly supernatural that so many around the world are sensitive and generous enough to keep us going financially.

We are also intensely grateful for so many of you who have taken on the ministry of intercession for us as we face many serious spiritual confrontations, crises and physical challenges. We know that the fruitfulness of our ministry is in answer to the love, faith and prayers of our Iris family around the world. Truly, we are a family, not a business, a management exercise or a political campaign. May you be richly, overwhelmingly blessed in return.

Boundless opportunities for missionary service with us exist in almost every area imaginable. As we encounter exploding hunger and respond on so many fronts, our need for expanded ministry and administrative infrastructure rises to match. Our missions school has almost doubled in size this session, but we are praying for help from any and every direction. Pour out your lives for Jesus. There is no other way to live!

For the One

Jesus gave His life for me,
He took away my pain,
He made beat this heart of mine
So I could love again.
In return I asked Him
What I could give away,
He showed me things
That break His heart,
And then I heard Him say.

Just stop for the one,
Until My Kingdom comes,
From the smallest seed,
Comes a mighty tree.
When you just stop for the one.

He showed me orphans on the street,
Their faces full of fear,
Always hungry, always cold,
Always death is near.
Girls in flimsy dresses,
Watching men drive past,
Trading on their kisses,
Every kiss their last.

He said . . .
Just stop for the one,
Until My Kingdom comes,
From the smallest seed,
Comes a mighty tree.
When you just stop for the one.

I saw boys without a purpose
Become men before their time.
Every day a little worse,
Driven into crime.
Drugs to ease the sorrow,
Never kill the pain,
Peace lasts 'til tomorrow,
Then it all starts up again.

Jesus stopped for children
And the thief on Calvary,
For the woman at the water well,
And then He stopped for me.
He said go love another,
Until the battle's done,
In this world you will have trouble,
But victory shall come.

He said . . .
Just stop for the one,
Until My Kingdom comes,
From the smallest seed
Comes a mighty tree.
Just stop for the one,
Until My will is done
Here on earth,
As you just . . . stop . . . for . . . the one.
Claire Vorster, 2012

Rolland and Heidi Baker are the founders and directors of Iris Ministries and have been missionaries for thirty years. They have taken deliberate steps to associate themselves with the world's poorest people and have become known for Heidi's policy of "stopping for the one." In other words, any human being in need is too important simply to pass by and do nothing. After spending many years ministering exclusively in Mozambique, Rolland and Heidi now travel internationally, teaching others about the simplicity of "passion and compassion" in the ministry of the Gospel. They have authored several books, including *Always Enough* and *Expecting Miracles*.

Rolland and Heidi began Iris Ministries in 1980. They were both ordained as ministers in 1985 after completing their B.A. and M.A. degrees at Vanguard University in Southern California. Sharing a heart for missions, they began by working with the poor in the slums of central Jakarta, Indonesia, and then among the forgotten street-sleepers and elderly in the most crowded urban area in the world: central Kowloon in Hong Kong. In 1992 they left Asia to earn Ph.D.s in systematic theology at King's College, University of London. At the same time they planted a warm and thriving church community for the homeless of downtown London. Then they were drawn to Mozambique, officially listed at the time as the poorest country in the world.

Alone and without support, they took over a horribly neglected and dilapidated orphanage in the capital of Mozambique, Maputo, with eighty orphans in rags. After improving the orphanage and expanding the ministry to 320 children, they were evicted by the government and lost everything. Then land was donated by a nearby city and they received provisions from all over the world. Graduates from the Bible school started by the Bakers went out and began healing the sick and raising the dead. Church growth in the bush exploded. When catastrophic flooding in 2000 brought torrential rain for forty days and nights, a cry for God rose up and their churches across the country multiplied into thousands.

Now Iris has networks of churches and church-based orphan care in all ten provinces in Mozambique, in addition to their bases in main cities. They lead missions training on the mission field, combining teaching, worship and spiritual impartation with everyday application to ministry among children and the poorest of the poor, both in towns and in the remote villages of the African bush.

To contact Heidi and Rolland Baker:

Iris Ministries
P.O. Box 493995
Redding, CA 96049-3995
530-255-2077
irisredding@irismin.org
www.irismin.org

More Inspiration from Heidi and Rolland Baker

During more than a decade of service in Mozambique, Rolland and Heidi Baker have witnessed countless miracles. Now they show you how you can have a part in the signs and wonders God is performing today. Combining extraordinary true stories with biblical insights and practical teaching, the Bakers offer priceless lessons on how God's power can transform your life.

Expecting Miracles

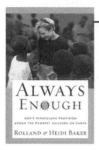

As you follow the adventures of the Bakers in Mozambique, you'll be awed by God's limitless power and tender provision. The account of how He has enabled them to help many thousands of Mozambique's children and start an astounding five thousand churches will warm your heart and move you to tears. Witness what God is doing in one of the poorest nations on earth in this book, and be assured that God's love and provision is always enough.

Always Enough

chosenbooks.com